LOVE IS THE DRUG

A mother and son memoir

Jodi Dale and Dane Jacobs

Dear Nancy,
I know you
will 'get' this
story. You are not
alone & I pray for
your son.
Love, jodi

To Dane who forever will be my heart and soul. The memory of our life together sustains me, and allows me to keep putting one foot in front of the other. I continue to draw from your courageous spirit every day. Until we can be together again, I love you my angel. Xo

This book could have never been written without my strong support system:

Randy, the best husband, friend, and stepdad in the world. Your support of Dane and I was above and beyond belief. Dane loved you so very much. And I'm forever your girl.

My Mom, my sister Lisa, and my brother Steve who loved Dane and were always available to listen to my teary voice.

Tony Smykla, for being the best friend Dane ever had. Please stop by anytime, we love you.

Cheryl, for the many hours of free therapy for both Dane and I.

Uncles Mark and Marty, who have been there from the beginning,.

Our friends, Kristin, Bob, and their family who took us in as one of their own.

Jeanne and Rose, for your constant support and love of Dane as well as Randy and I.

Beautiful Michelle, who originally believed I could write.

Mark Durfee, my friend and wonderful editor who encouraged Dane and I on writing in 2011. Thank you for everything. This book would not happen without your encouragement, not to mention correcting my silly slang and for indulging my irrational love of the semi-colon.

Charles, Erik, and Jim; my blog friends and supporters of the blog I have been writing for the past 8 years.

Dr. Aala Mansour, the most supportive, sympathetic, and loving doctor I've ever known. Thank you for going above and beyond the call of duty for our family.

Donna Major, who has shown me that there is still light in the day again and to understand that even in grief love lives on.

Tom Thompson, the one who patiently walked me through my computer issues.

Anthony Rinaldi, the creative genius behind the book cover.

If I've left out anyone, please forgive me.

All my love

Jodi

I answered the phone one day in 2011, something I am not in the habit of doing, and it was my friend Jodi. She talked for a minute before she said the words I remember; meet, coffee, questions, and idea. Trust me when I say those words are magnetic for me, especially coffee. When we met she had her son Dane with her, a man about half my age I had never met before. The idea was to write a book, how to get started, how to format and the other technical issues in just sitting down and getting the ideas out on paper. The information given over the phone was not enough at the moment but then Dane started to tell me his story; he was forthright about his past, recent, and for years back. I didn't know then what I know now, his history of mental illness, the Bi-polar condition; but I did recognize a manic state where the mind and the words are just rushing out, subject matter changing at a pace that seemed to me that any information I could offer would never take root. As I said I did not know Dane Jacobs and how intelligent he truly was.

That meeting was my only encounter with Dane and from that encounter this book has risen. After the first reading of the completed manuscript I admit openly I was truly touched. Then out came the editor's eye, seeing beyond the emotion and looking at the work. I care for Jodi very much; I felt deeply her pain and grief as I too have lost a few friends over the years in the same way she lost her son. But with each run through the writing became easier to look at impersonally, the same as I do with every edit I take on.

I took on the work for two reasons, the first being my feeling for Jodi and Randy and the second because it is a story that needs to be told. Other families and friends of families who are going through the same problems of a very deficient mental health system that even with the Affordable Care Act, still lingers on today (2016). Insurance that is only bottom line oriented, and self-medication leading to the death or near death of a loved one. Hopefully within these pages are insight and a way to deal correctly with the double edge sword of mental health and drug abuse.

Any errors in the edit are mine and mine alone. Had it not been for the subject matter, working with Jodi has been a pleasure.

"Strength does not come from physical capacity. It comes from an indomitable will." Mahatma Gandhi

Mark C Durfee
bdd44m5@gmail.com

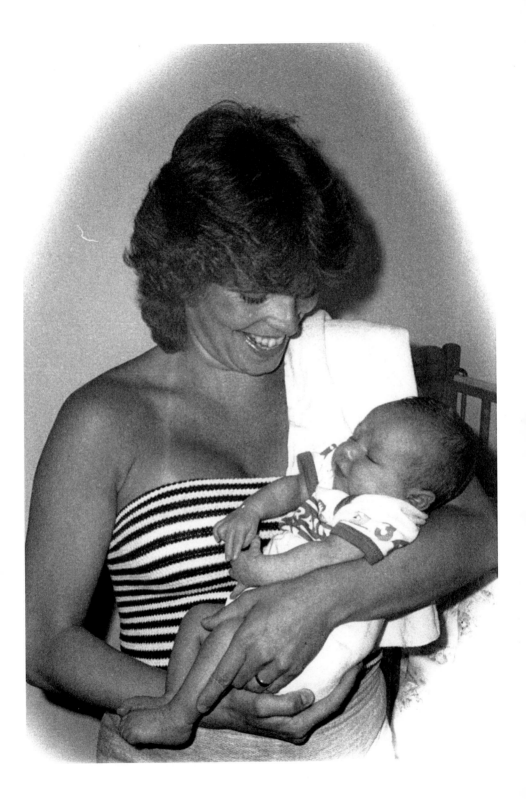

TABLE OF CONTENTS

Editing: Mark C Durfee

ISBN:9781530637881

Printed in the United States of America

Author and publisher Jodi Dale

jodidale69@gmail.com

FORWARD

I need to share with you the reason I feel compelled to tell this story. The day I had my only child Dane, was the happiest day of my life. He was nothing less than a perfect miracle and the absolute light of my world. Being a nursing mother, he was literally attached to me for the first year of his life. A special connection was forged and our strong bond was never broken. As a single mother, he simply was my reason for living. As a beautiful baby, a curious toddler, a complicated teen, and a troubled adult, Dane was always my best friend. In his to short life, he impacted many others as well. His sense of humor and warmth along with his incredible intellect brought smiles to everyone he interacted with. His struggles were my struggles, and it crushed me to be unable to fix his world.

Dane and I started this project together in 2011 with the intent being to create a very accurate account of all that we had been through. Sitting at my kitchen bar with our steaming coffee mugs and open laptops, we endeavored to tell the tale. The original story would have been from both of our perspectives during the same time frame. It was intended to be more of a cautionary tale with Dane's side of the story being a personal recall of his mental illness and addiction, while I told of the experience from the angle of a parent living with and learning about these issues. Without a doubt, this would have been a very gritty and colorful story with Dane's recall of the progression of his diseases. But, after completing five chapters Dane expressed some trepidation. He was having trouble continuing. His side of the story was going to take a very dark turn as he had done things he was ashamed of. Because we had decided to tell the absolute truth, he backed away from the project. Randy suggested that we put him back in therapy hoping that he could work through some of these issues and feel free to continue writing, unashamed of his truth. Dane agreed and plunged into his sessions to be able to face things and honestly write about them.

But that was not how things would work out. He helped me with some outlines and remembered some incidents and dates, but did not actually write another chapter. It is only because of some of his memories that I was able to recall the facts as vividly. However, writing the rest of this story by myself, the color of it has changed a little. My wish is to help other parents that find themselves in this horrific situation. Or maybe a person that is struggling will see themselves and realize that they are not alone. Hopefully, our experience and resources will be applicable to their lives. The things I've seen, learned and battled for-I would never trade. Dane was worth every moment and every single effort. It is now my hope to tell this story as both a love song, and a tribute to my precious son.

Dane's painful life had meaning and purpose even amidst his struggles. If I can reach even one person, and help in any way, he and I will have accomplished what together, we set out to do. My heart is missing the piece that made me complete and I am forever changed because of his death. I realize that this book will be a struggle for me to get through, but it is a labor of love and I welcome the opportunity to revisit the good times as well as the bad.

And I love you Dane-today and always. May you enjoy peace and find your joy until we can be together again. Always your Mom and Poppy. Xo

June 2015

As I hurried across the parking lot, my focus was on a quick 'Target run'. I'll just hurry in, grab a few things and be on my way, determined not to get sucked into the 'Target vortex" and spend hours buying everything *but* the things on my list.

Approaching the door, I noticed a boy, maybe 25 years of age, walking toward me pulling a small suitcase. My eyes locked with his and I couldn't turn away. I instantly recognized the look that spelled deep despair. It was obvious to me that he was in very serious trouble. The pale skin and tired eyes were a dead giveaway. "Excuse me ma'am, do you have any change for the bus?" I did but I wanted to see something first. "Show me your arms." I demanded. He sighed and rolled up his sleeves to reveal fresh, as well as old track marks. "How long have you been using?" I asked. "3 years. I started out with OxyContin and it led to snorting heroin. A year ago I started on the needle. I'm on a waiting list to get into a rehab."

I caught my breath and pulled out my wallet to show him the picture that I will always carry with me. "This is my son, Dane." I told him. Peering at the picture, his face lit up. "Hey, I know him! We were in Sacred Heart together. How's he doing?"

With my eyes swimming in tears, I told him. "Dane is no longer here. He overdosed one year ago."

"Oh man that's too bad, he was cool we had some good talks in rehab, but I really need to catch my bus"

I was so close to a complete meltdown in the parking lot that I simply reached into my purse grabbed a five and handed it over and choked out the words, "get yourself something to eat please."

It was a snowy, winter afternoon when I was putting away laundry in Dane's room that I caught the distinct odor of marijuana. No mistaking that skunky odor. What the hell? My son doesn't smoke grass. Well, if he does, I'm going to find it-right here and right now. I glanced around his neat room and wondered where to start my search. Turns out I didn't have to look too far. On top of the desk, where the smell was the strongest, sat an incense burner, in plain sight. And, boy did it smell. Dane, you dumb ass, didn't you even have the brains to hide it? I flipped open the lid and sure enough, there was the baggies and the rolling papers and a small amount of pot. Deep breath here-heart pounding a little. Exhale. Okay, well I grew up in the seventies and pot was not new to me. And really, wouldn't I have seen some signs if he was in trouble? Red eyes, slurred speech, or the smell on his clothing? SOMETHING? Guess he was just better at hiding it than we were. Visine and Febreze are no brainers and what teenager tells his parents everything anyway?

And after all, Dane was 15 years old and it was 1998 and Lord knows there were much more dangerous drugs out there. And technically, marijuana isn't even a real drug. Willie Nelson taught everybody that grass is well, just grass. A weed, actually. At least he wasn't coming home falling down drunk every weekend. Dane was a gifted student and very grade driven. He even had plans to follow his Uncle Steve into the field of dentistry. It really can't be that big of a deal, right? I will confront him after school, tell Randy after dinner, and be assured that this little family talk will prevent the situation from getting out of hand. And that he will NEVER smoke or bring dope into this house. And I will be watching very closely. After all I was only 40 and I wasn't born yesterday. I knew what to look for. Right?

If only I could have known that the rollercoaster ride had just begun, I may not have had the attitude towards pot that I had as a teenager. Our love would be tested and tried, and pushed to the maximum of human patience and understanding.

Randy and I would learn at first blindly, and then with many episodes and classes we earned an education. We would become unlikely experts in the many classes of narcotic drugs, as well as eye opening street experiences.

We would become all too familiar with mental health disease and the hospitals and rehabs that treat it. It would become an immense financial strain. At first we would ride hoping the ride would end soon until we would learn to hold on tight through the bumps and corners found in love, fighting addiction, and the ways and means of insurance coverage or lack thereof. Not only would we attempt to guide Dane through his personal struggles, we would fight tooth and nail to have his mental illness be recognized and treated like the serious, life threatening disease that it is.

Randy and I would endeavor to stay in love and love Dane-as hard as he was at times to love. Granted, you always will love your child, but fighting the addiction coupled with a mental illness was like running a 26-mile marathon on one foot. It would prove to be a long race with many, many hard falls. Our relationship as a family would be tested to very nearly snapping. But learning and loving would help us through the unbelievable world of both drug addiction and mental illness. Love and only love, would let us survive.

At some times of utter frustration at a lack of a logical explanation for it all, I find myself wishing that I'd had a bad childhood. One rife with hardships or physical and emotional abuse, or that I had experienced some deeply scarring sort of trauma. After all, how could my loving and romanticized perfect youth be the breeding ground for chronic mental illness and drug addiction? Why can't I cite a reason for all of this, and how can so many people who did experience those situations lead lives so much more fruitful than mine? As a person who struggles with illogic and generally seeks a direct, straight-line answer to every problem, these are two questions that keep me staring at the ceiling at night. What the fuck?

Sure, I came from a broken home. Yes, I was teased as a child. Naturally, the uprooting from my hometown was difficult. But for most people of my generation this is simply par for the course. For any painful memory I can instantly think of a hundred cherished ones that overwhelmingly trump anything negative. Not to mention, I was intelligent, athletic, and reasonably well liked by most people. School always came easily to me, up to college, that is. I typically did well at any sport that I had the self-confidence to play and also became very physically fit weightlifting in my teens and early twenties. Though I was never overly popular I usually got along fairly well with my peers barring a few exceptions when I was bullied in my younger days. My parents, though separated, always made it known that they loved me dearly. And being the only child and grandchild in my family I received far more than my fair share of attention.

Mom was simply amazing, she worked so hard and made so many sacrifices to provide me with every opportunity she could. Dad came and went for long periods at a time, and my first clear memory of him seems to be when I was approximately nine years old, but when he was around we had fun together. He absolutely could have been there more for me no doubt. His father passed away suddenly when he was ten years old and I have often resolved any animosities by concluding that since he lacked a father from early on it was difficult for him to understand his role as a dad. Grandpa however provided me with a wonderful father figure; I remember thinking as a kid that he was totally indestructible, and nearly infallible at that. Standing 6'3" with a strong, big-boned frame, he was undoubtedly the strongest man on Earth at that time. Mom and I lived with her parents for a few years, from as early as I could remember until I was about seven years old if I'm correct, and it was all good times composed of staying up too late and Grandma's exquisite baking. There were only a few other kids my age in the neighborhood, but we lived in a small, quaint rural village suburb within walking distance of our elementary school. It was a ten street grid covering maybe a hundred acres, and we felt like we owned it all, or up to the borders of U.S. 23 and Nicholson Hill Road anyway. All of the games were two-on-two given the lack of players and we could play whatever sport in whichever neighbor's yard best accommodated it. Our little lives played out within a quarter mile radius from the house that I eventually shared with Mom at the veritable center of the suburb. They were blissful, halcyon days lifted directly from the pages of D.H. Lawrence.

That is not to say that this utopian vision was without fault. Without a solid father figure, coupled with a combined smaller stature and larger intellect, I was the prime subject for bullying.

I would fight back when I could but over time I developed deep anxieties related to verbal and physical abuse. Conflict sparked very strong fight of flight reactions. There were days when I would lock myself in my room and completely avoid the normal daily contact with the neighborhood guys. In junior high I would fake sick to avoid two older kids who strove to make my days' hell. I'm not sure I ever would have used one under any circumstances, but on a few occasions I would bring a knife to school with me, and I certainly did romanticize stabbing and slitting throats at will. Aside from a few, most of whom were in a similar position, my peers became my enemies. I became hyper vigilant and obsessive regarding threats. Today I still suffer with these same fears, anxieties and quick overreacting triggers to anger or defense.

It can easily be argued that Dane could have been under some stress. It was only last year that I uprooted him from the small town of Ossineke, Michigan and moved him to Harrison Twp., a suburb outside of Detroit. Randy and I had been alternating weekend commutes and the 229.9 mile round trip was wearing us both out. We were very serious in our relationship and completely vested in our future.

We knew that living together as a family was the next logical step. When we made this decision on New Year's Day, it was a day I will never forget. Randy and I had spent the weekend in the Upper Peninsula where we celebrated the New Year's Eve with friends at a cabin. It was one of the snowiest holidays I can ever remember. The beauty of the Upper was even more so when blanketed in 3 feet of snow with big, soft, downy flakes lazily floating down. Holiday lights went from mediocre to awesome under the frosty glow.

Walking into Tahquamenon Falls was like entering into a crystal fairy tale. The trees were heavy with sparkly snow and the falls in winter were breathtaking. It was easy to make resolutions and promise to keep them with this astounding natural spectacle as a background. It was 'God's country' and his beautiful creation reminded us that all things were possible. With deep, breaths of the cold, crisp air, I vowed to always be present in this secure, loving, and comfortable life.

The future was as heavy with promise as the 6-foot snow banks that lined the roads as we headed back over the Mackinaw Bridge. The radio news station had on Randy and I appalled as some sketchy details of the Jon Benet Ramsey murder came to light. It was a horrific contrast to all that was going on in our world that day. I'll never forget learning of that little girl's death. Randy quickly changed the channel from the news saying that today is a special day and some nice music would be more in keeping with our current mood. We would allow 'reality' to re-enter soon enough. Chrissy Hyne singing "I'll Stand by You", was a much better and more fitting accompaniment to our day. The sun was blindingly bright and Randy and I slid on our sunglasses as we prepared to pay the toll and cross over the bridge to resume our lives like the 'trolls' that the 'yooper's' accused us of being.

As Randy and I carefully maneuvered across the icy 'Mighty Mack' on that gorgeous day and decided that we would merge all 3 of our lives, we had no idea what a slippery, tenuous slope we would be asked to navigate. But love would be the thing, the glue, the ideal that we would keep clinging to as we tried to saved Dane's life and keep our lives whole.

I distinctly remember the day when my mother told me we were moving to the city. It literally hit me in the chest with far more force than any of the comparatively weak childhood blows I had taken. For minutes I could not breathe, move, or think. It's amazing what details the mind stores during times of dramatic trauma or stress.

One specific memory is a glass of Nestle Quick that I was drinking, it sat on our glass coffee table in front of the couch. As we sat, while mom spoke and I remained a non-participant in the discussion, the mixture separated and lost its homogenous properties. Even at the time, this seemingly minor development symbolized the change that was due to occur, two layers representing the old and the new times in my life.

This image still comes to mind at times of distress. Life wasn't great, but it certainly wasn't bad either. Even the aspects that I hated, the primary constituents being anyone near my age who posed competition or a threat, were devils that I at least knew.

I've always feared change of any sort as does anyone with a bent toward worst case scenario thought. This tiny crossroads village, with its nearby sleepy city, was all that I had ever known. My life so far had taken place in a rural vacuum with very few excursions elsewhere.

With my love of the outdoors and solitude, I had no problem with this. The bombshell idea of moving to a suburb of Detroit represented a complete destruction of life as I knew it, a trade of imperfection for the intolerable.

When the time came it seemed like we just jumped in the car and left. Mom and I had so few belongings worth taking to my stepfather's already established home.

To his great credit, my stepfather Randy did his best to make the transition as smooth as possible. It was summertime, I had just turned 13, and school didn't start for another three months. We lived on a dead-end street with only about six kids my age. There was definitely a period of assimilation, but after a while it didn't feel all that different from my hermetic Ossineke existence.

Life occurred in a bubble that was far sheltered from what I was later to experience in the actual Detroit; this being much closer to the life I had envisioned.

School soon began, and many of my fears materialized when my summertime friends scattered into their respective impenetrable cliques, leaving me to my familiar worst case scenario. I walked the halls and sat in the cafeteria alone. Eventually I made a few friends who also orbited the fringes, but the clash of cultures between Northern Michigan and the chic suburbs was painfully evident.

My wardrobe lacked the branding or pricing to make me eligible for any semblance of popularity. Left with little else to concentrate on, and with a practiced disinterest in anything extra-curricular, I focused solely on my schoolwork. Even with advanced classes making the honor roll soon became a given rather than an accomplishment. I became accustomed to expecting this easy success, something that never seemed like it would exact the toll that was to come in later years.

I was very pleased that Dane would be attending L'Anse Creuse High School, a highly rated, college prep orientated school. He had always earned exemplary grades and would now have the chance to continue on his educational goal of graduation and then college. It was likely that he would meet friends with like aspirations to study and hang out with. Our hopes were high and Dane did not disappoint. Even with advanced and college prep classes, his grades were at the top. As an elementary student, I never had to get after him to do his homework. He was always self-motivated and was harder on himself than we would ever be. His perfectionist manner proved stronger than ever and parent-teacher conferences confirmed this. Dane was a model student. In grade school Dane was always winning a writing contest of some sort, so it was no surprise when his A.P. English teacher told Randy and I that he was a very gifted writer and should probably pursue his talent. But, he never had confidence in his writing and had to be convinced that it was something of value. I, however, loved that praise and secretly-and not so secretly-hoped it would somehow happen someday.

At 2:30 when L'Anse Creuse High School ended it was a flood of kids rushing out to end their school day. Dane was certainly among the crowd hurrying home to kick back and have himself a snack. He could make it home quickly and burst thru the door at 2:32 that day, the day I found his pot. I was laying for him. The poor kid could barely drop his backpack when I said, "how come I have to find pot in your room? Where did you get it? And don't bother to tell me that it's not yours!"

"Oh, yeah, he says, it's mine. I smoke a little from time to time. Don't worry about where I get it, it's safe." "Well", I replied, "it's not okay. You are too young and pot is not allowed in our home. Hitting someone's joint is one thing, buying it from someone I don't know and bringing it home is quite another." "Really, Mom?" he says, "You're making a big deal out of nothing. All my friends smoke a bit and we take turns buying and splitting it. Sheesh! Take it easy, man."

"Don't tell me to take it easy. I'm telling Randy tonight after work and he can help me deal with you." By now, Dane had grabbed an apple and a large hunk of cheese and was headed upstairs to his room to relax before tackling his homework. At least that's one thing I didn't ever have to worry about. He was a self-starter and did all school work thoughtfully and without fail. He was slated for Honor Roll in this, his first year of high school, and a new school at that. His friends-at least the ones we met-were on the same fast track to college. Many times, we hosted the study party where they would help each other thru their A.P. classes or create funny skits for Spanish class.

I loved having his friends around and would often deliver bowls of hot, buttered popcorn and Crystal Lite to them. It was hard to not feel a little smug where Dane's academics were concerned.

He was also approached by both the football and lacrosse coaches to try out for the teams. I would have loved him to get involved, but he said with studies and going back up north to see family and friends, that he wouldn't really have time. He was always a great athlete excelling in basketball, baseball and bowling. But no amount of my reasoning could change his mind. We would have to understand I guess; besides he told us that he would rather find a job and start saving for a car. Okay, I thought, your choice.

That night after dinner, I told Randy of our afternoon conversation and asked what he thought was appropriate. We decided that if his grades were maintained, he would be allowed to work part time. Randy re-affirmed the rules about the pot and asked Dane to consider what the future implication of drugs could do to his life. He did assure us that he had no interest in any other drug. Okay, status quo, for the time being.

I will never forget the first time that I crossed the 8 Mile border headed south on Mound Road. Granted the southern areas of Warren are no paradise, but when you step over that line it really is a shock. This is still as true today as it was 15 years ago. At age fourteen I was beginning my eventually lengthy work history at a construction supply company located at McNichols and Conant streets in an area northeast of the hamlet of Hamtramck.

It also stands to mention that Highland Park, an isolated city within the city of Detroit, was nearby. While Hamtramck was known for the established Polish community and lovable eccentricities like safe neighborhoods and great food, Highland Park, was infamous for being bankrupt and hence possibly the single most undesirable place to live in the entire Detroit region.

Pulling into that dirt parking lot was like driving onto one of the moons of Mars. It was, in a word, fucked.

The facility consisted of two dilapidated brick buildings with a rutty unpaved parking lot in between. Through the barbed wire fencing laid a completely defunct alley backing up to either abandoned homes or those whose owners had simply lost the will to stand against the encroaching blight. These houses were difficult to tell from the empty ones as each had people standing on porches and boards over some windows. It was also my first exposure to black people in any concentration, Detroit being over 90% black after all. Most of the northern suburban affinities towards racism seemed to be confirmed in my young mind, which at the time had yet to assimilate many of the other factors that could lead to these ways of life.

Thus came my first direct exposure to alcohol and drugs. Everyone that I worked with either drank, smoked weed, or got high somehow on the job. Picking up weed at a nearby house and smoking it outside of the third bay door seemed to be the order of the day. For some, the routine consisted of shooting heroin in the bathroom, nodding out at the welding station, or catching a nap on one of the upper shelves where there were "beds" consisting of cardboard and a few rags.

I never witnessed anybody shooting up and only later did it become completely obvious that it was happening. It still never crossed my mind to even entertain trying it, thought the alcohol and weed did seem appealing.

My overprotective coworkers were oddly enthusiastic about my first times getting high.

I smoked with them and rode home with Randy stoned as shit. The friendly local ghetto liquor store was all too happy to sell me the occasional bottle for cash. There wasn't any peer pressure, and it felt like I was just doing what everyone else did.

That summer, I surpassed almost anybody I knew in the realms of what I perceived as worldly knowledge. It was a baptism that would have consequences and impacts on almost every aspect of my life, then and now.

The next three years went by in a blur. Dane started a summer job, at 14 years old. For the next three summers, three days a week, Randy and Dane rode together to work, coffee mugs in hand. The company Randy managed was a small family owned business that sold commercial construction supplies. It was located at McNichols and Conant in Detroit on the fringe of Hamtramck. When the company opened some thirty years ago, the area was in much better shape with many different businesses directly surrounding the O.L. Johnson Company. The original Buddy's Pizza, a Detroit staple, is still right across the street. I was worried about my son working there with guys much older and certainly much more experienced than him.

The whole area provided him quite a massive culture shock, to say the least. Thank God long time secretary, Jeanne was there. She took Dane under her wing and kept a good eye on him. They connected immediately and she is counted as one of his very best friends for life. I knew that there was the usual amount of pot and alcohol used by some of the guys, but I did not feel that Dane was in any particular danger. Most of the guys were very protective of the 'boss man's son'. And Dane was still very solidly rooted in his conviction to work for a vehicle and make good grades to help with a college scholarship.

Life was quite peaceful during that time. Dane passed his drivers training and the summer of his sixteenth birthday, was able to purchase a two-year-old Chevrolet Sonoma pickup. He had savings bonds from past birthdays that we were able to cash in to add to his down payment and Randy and I floated him a loan for the balance. Dane paid us fifty dollars a month toward his debt as well as fifty dollars a month for his insurance.

Without fail, every month he would proudly hand over the cash and watch closely as I updated his loan balance. We both felt very proud and he looked so cute driving off in his truck, stereo blasting. Even though we lived a short walk from the school, Dane still drove his truck every day.

Having the ability to drive made it possible for him to secure employment at Powerhouse Gym, which is located about three miles from our home. Dane would zip home, grab a snack and his black Powerhouse Gym t-shirt and head out to work. He was generally assigned simple janitorial duties, but with some training, graduated to working the floor and answering questions regarding the weight machines and training form. In the slow times, he was allowed to get his own workout in.

He told me he had a crush on the cute girl that worked at the counter and hoped to sometime ask her out. Before too long, his lean body took on a much more muscular shape. In his tight t-shirt that showed off his big biceps and 'six pack', there was no doubt that he lived the life. Arriving home just after 9:00 p.m., Dane would eat dinner and head up to his room to finish his homework.

During this same time period, he landed a weekend job at Mac n Ray's, an upscale eatery on Lake St. Clair. Again, the commute was approximately a 3-mile drive. The restaurant is a gorgeous behemoth of a building located at the MacRay Harbor. With 300 boat slips, a pool and 30 'dockaminiums', the place was always jumping. There were reception rooms downstairs where weddings and such were held and an upstairs area that featured the main dining room. The view was incredible overlooking the lake and the harbor. Huge yachts, in every slip complimented the scene. It was a very popular restaurant with crisply uniformed waiters, waitresses and various servers that were pretty much running their butts off.

Dane was not old enough to serve liquor and was assigned to be a food runner. And run he did! Randy and I loved to have dinner there and watch him work. He carried out large trays of food while dodging people headed to the dance floor where an always fabulous band could be heard. He then set up trays for the waiters and ran back for whatever they had forgotten.

He didn't always love that job, but he sure did love the money. When he got home from work, we always waited for him to tell us his 'war stories' as well as roll out that wad of cash. And what a wad of cash it was! It was not unusual for him to have pocketed over $150.00 dollars in tips for a four-hour shift. That didn't even include his paycheck which seemed incidental after the tip money. He stayed at that job for a couple of years easily paying off his truck and buying himself pretty much whatever he wanted.

He saw many local minor celebrities and amused us with stories of their eating, drinking and dancing. He looked forward to seeing Anna Kournikova and Sergei Fedorov when they docked their boat and came into the restaurant for the Sunday buffet. That job proved to be a pretty enlightening experience for a boy from northern Michigan. He later dropped the Powerhouse Gym job. His classes were getting harder and he felt that he needed more time to study. The weekend job provided more than enough money to pay his bills. And he always had summer and school vacations to go to work with Randy.

Impossibly, junior year in high school was upon us. Dane had made the Honor Roll every marking period in his freshman and sophomore year. Junior year would be no different even with the tough class load he was carrying. On the weekend that he would be taking his A.C.T.'s, my parents would be coming down for a visit. My Dad was helping us to install a hardwood floor in our home office.

On Friday night, we read over what to expect from the A.C.T. testing day. It was advised that Dane eat a good dinner and try to get as much sleep as possible the night before. I made sure he ate breakfast before heading out to school. The testing would begin at eight a.m. and would last approximately four or five hours. We were all having coffee as we wished him good luck. "No big deal", he said, "See you soon."

Randy and I and Mom and Dad got busy working on the floor. Two hours later I thought I heard Dane's truck pull in. My heart sunk as I thought something had surely gone wrong. I needn't have worried. He burst thru the door and the look on my face must have lead him to explain. "I'm done. Finished the test. Really wasn't that hard." Oh my God. "You mean to tell me that you didn't study for the test and you are DONE?" "Yeah, Mom, I was the first one finished, so I got to split. What's for lunch?"

Needless to say, Dane had no problem graduating with honors. It was a very proud moment when he was awarded his diploma with various honor cords. We were near to busting buttons with pride. After the ceremony, Randy and I were all set to have a family celebratory dinner. Dane insisted that White Castle was more of what he had in mind.

Plans to hook up with some friends later were much more important that watching Pops and Mom toast their good luck. So, we got him a 'crave case' before we proceeded to Luigi's for our dinner. His A.C.T. being one of the highest scores in his class making him eligible for scholarship money. All that was left was his transition to college.

To any outsider and upon my own refection, things went quite well for most of my late teens. I had three jobs depending on the time of year; I worked at a local gym, and upscale restaurant of Lake St. Clair, and full time summers at O.L. Johnson. The gym provided me with a bit of side income during my junior and senior years of high school along with a free membership, the restaurant provided me a constant source of instant cash, and OLJ provided a respectable income with easy access to drugs and alcohol.

Yes, I did work my ass off, and yes I did save enough money to build a respectable savings account for a car and college. Yet at the same time I was blowing money on everything from partying to stereo equipment to any other frivolity I really desired. It really fulfilled the cliché of working hard and playing harder. When I look back upon this time I often regard it as the happiest period of my life. They were golden years, and the good ol' days; the sun was shining and I was making hay.

God, did I fuck off the job at the gym. My only qualifications at the time were being in peak physical condition and having the willingness to wipe the asses of arrogant muscle-heads who were way too busy doing steroids to actually clean up after themselves. Over time I moved from janitor to a very unofficial trainer of new members.

The legality of this could be questioned, but it beat the hell out of mopping out the men's shower or plunging the perpetually plugged toilets. High protein diets and power squats never mix. Eventually, after a few complaints were fielded from the more respected and thus bitchier members, the owner reviewed a tape of a week's worth of my work. The average 5-hour shift would have ideally been spent patrolling the training floor, maintaining machinery, re-racking weights, and keeping the place in general order.

The odd training assignment was mercifully thrown in maybe once a shift and normally occupied approximately forty-five minutes depending on the (lack of) physical condition of the new member. However, upon examination it was revealed that my given tasks were accomplished as hastily as possible and were typically reduced to about 25% of my time on the clock. Making myself free protein shakes, unsuccessfully chatting up the counter girl, and completing an extensive workout regimen occupied the remainder. I quit the job not long after that stern warning. Working at the gym was far too much actual work for the money.

The money I made at the restaurant was ridiculous for someone my age. It wasn't out of the ordinary to bring home $200 cash or more on a busy weekend in addition to the thirty odd hours at minimum wage. Most of us were under 18, thereby constituting a grievous breach of labor laws, given our long shifts and late hours, but nobody was about to bitch. It's not like a bunch of high school kids were going to form a labor union.

On a good night I could easily take home more than the busiest/cutest waitress there. It was criminal to work there and criminal insanity to quit. Free time for your other friends was definitely limited but, much like OLJ, there were plenty of drugs to use while working.

Being the dogsbodies of the operation meant that we were often there the latest. Adrenaline fuels the restaurant business; the pace is fast, the mind must be ultra-focused to handle the multi-tasking, and tempers often flare. Cap it off with the euphoric rush of receiving a large amount of cash, and it becomes difficult to simply drift off to sleep upon returning home.

My coworkers and I would drag race the relatively long distance of the driveway from the restaurant to the road, then meet up at whatever pre-planned destination to divvy up our drugs and alcohol in accordance with preference and tolerance. Inevitably cleaning up someone's vomit, we'd watch the sun come up knowing that we had another grueling shift looming in eight hours away. Monday became our new Sabbath.

On June 06, 2001 Dane turned 18. Plans for him to start at University of Detroit Mercy were finalized and moving day took place on a balmy August morning.

U. of D. is a small Jesuit college located in Detroit, specializing in premed and law. It was approximately 20 miles from our home, a distance that made me comfortable. One of our employees was enrolled and was instrumental in getting Dane interested in pursuing his degree there. Andy had introduced Dane to some of the activities available and even encouraged him to join a fraternity.

We made lists, bought supplies and books and packed his things. Campus was in frenzy as the new freshman class was setting up in the dorms. As we pulled up, with the truck packed to the gills, the U. of D. moving committee directed us and helped us unload. Dane's new roommate was a friend from high school so the transition was to be a bit easier saving him some of the usual new roommate anxiety. We beat Ray in arriving, so we got to choose the bunk and closet area and made quick work of setting up Dane's new home. Soon after, Ray arrived and the two chatted excitedly about the year to come.

Randy and I took this as our cue to leave. Dane walked us down to the truck. As hugs went around our circle, I could feel the lump in my throat forming. As we drove off, I turned around and saw our son, standing alone, waving goodbye. He was on his own, and for the first time ever, we would be apart. The choices would be his-for better or worse. I would no longer be there as his watchdog and confidant. The finality of the situation hit me hard, and I burst into tears.

The rest of the summer and fall flew by with Randy being busier than ever at work. I was still working part time at the salon and enjoyed my interactions with both the girls I worked with as well as my customers. Two days a week provided me lots of free time to hit the gym and still be able to organize our lives.

Dane seemed to adjusting well and making lots of new friends that appeared as goal oriented as he. We were proud to say that our son was at University of Detroit Mercy studying to be a dentist. It was a very contented time for Randy and I although the house was very quiet as empty nests tend to be. I sorely missed his daily presence and it was all I could do not to call him to often. With incredible willpower from me, fact that he was a 'Mama's boy' would be kept a secret!

The year went on quite uneventfully with the exception of Randy and I buying our dream home in the Florida Keys. We had been visiting the Keys for years and an opportunity to purchase a condominium became a reality for us. Our friends had a place there and invited us to join them on a vacation. We fell in love with the place, which is situated on the ocean on Long Key.

With some financial finagling, we were the proud owners of a three bedroom, townhouse style condo. The former owner explained how renting out the place could help with the expenses. We happily booked many renters, saving a few weeks a year for ourselves to visit. Our Keys home provided much joy and stress relief for years to come. It was and still is a relaxing haven for us.

By this time, OLJ and the surrounding ghetto had become familiar territory. The winos, junkies and crackheads considered outcasts by the rest of society had become integrated within my group of associates. They accurately assessed my comparatively lucrative job and my noticeably white skin, thus making me out to be the easy mark that I was.

Everyone within a mile radius knew that we all cashed our checks like clockwork every Thursday morning at our 10:00 a.m. break. Sweet it was to be alive those Thursday mornings. Our weed spot was a few minutes away; it's a drive I could make today even after 15 years. Week after week, year after year, we went to the same house and bought everyone's weekly supply.

The only thing that ever changed was the steadily increasing quantity that we purchased. A $20 one eighth ounce bag used to last me at least a week. I was eventually picking up an ounce for $120 to tide me over for the same period. Some of it I sold, and a lot of it I smoked with friends, but the lion's share went to me alone. Getting high at work meant that I now often stayed stoned all day, for days at a time.

Societally speaking, drugs represented my views on two fronts. I was rebelling and satisfying my wayward teen angst by getting high, at the same time I was conforming by doing what my coworkers and friends were doing. Neither argument is completely logical but perpetually stoned teenagers really can't be bothered by giving a fuck about such trivialities. I had my reasons and they were justifiable enough for me. Anyone who disagreed didn't "understand" me, or "didn't know where I was coming from", maaaan.

Plus, I was generally advancing in the world. These facts also helped to nullify any argument presented by authority figures. Weed and alcohol were in all likelihood not assisting in this advancement, however, they also seemed to be a very minor prohibitive factor.

Even as an elementary school student, I had a proclivity for arguing against those who bandied around terms such as "gateway drug" or anything related to organized religion. People also have a tendency to default to these blanket explanations when presented with inconvenient little refutes, such as logic. People also have a tendency to get thoroughly pissed off when their classrooms or catechism lessons are interrupted by some bastard kid lawyering on their own behalves.

I thereby formed the opinion that people had a tendency to not know shit. This revelation thoroughly pleased me because I thought that if everybody else was wrong than I must be right. I was too young and naive to see that I had just placed myself into the group who used those blanket explanations that I hated. It seems important to state this as a sort of footnote here because I obviously carried this view into my teen and forthcoming adult years.

I wouldn't reevaluate this view until much later in my life, and by that time it was already too late. The wheels of cause and effect were set in motion by a child, and would only begin to come full circle some ten years later when I was preparing to enter adulthood.

The individual times that I tried new drugs all stick out in my mind, and they're all fond memories. Most drug abusers will tell you that at first, before the spiral into addiction or dependence, the drugs helped them.

I know they helped me. If it weren't for alcohol I may still be a virgin. Pot relaxed me, showed me a lighter side of life, and kept me off hard drugs for a long time. Ecstasy strengthened the bonds that I already had with my life-long friends. That's all the deeper I got into drugs during this idealistic stage of my life. Fuck it, I had kicked high school's ass, I was accepted on a scholarship to a prestigious university in the dental field, and I was making more money than I could spend. I just worked hard and played hard.

Charlie B.

Charlie B. has filthy days

Charlie B. has grimy ways.

Ice and milk won't suffice

the fiends for dirty vice.

Chasing fake mice

Left for last

Chore Boy blast.

It's half past

a rat's ass

Through the glass.

Don't give him one

on credit

Don't let him come and get it.

He knows right where to put it.

A candle and a blanket,

Take a hit and forget it.

©Dane Jacobs

(I learned via an internet search that "Charlie B." is urban slang or Mexican Brown heroin.)

Boxed

Boxed inside these convenient walls of reason

My will has died.

Lack of security removes me from almost any possibility

Left to wonder but thankful to imagine what may lie under

or what may be in.

Try to eliminate any allusion towards my state

towards my state

towards my allusion

created by desire

unable to combine the opposite vectors

of heart and mind

My own surroundings force me to let her

keep bleeding me

Fears of change, fears of failure are the stage

That I live through

If I can't be what I want

than at least it is even if it will only haunt

what normally glitters.
©Dane Jacobs

(found in an old college notebook amidst class notes for biology)

A Happy Baby

UNITED STATES OF AMERICA

STATE OF MICHIGAN
DEPARTMENT OF COMMUNITY HEALTH
CERTIFICATE OF DEATH

LF
CF 1653

STATE FILE NUMBER
3743018

1. DECEDENT'S NAME (First, Middle, Last)		2. DATE OF BIRTH (Month, Day, Year)	3. SEX	4. DATE OF DEATH (Month, Day, Year) On or After
Dane Andrew Jacobs		June 6, 1983	Male	June 3, 2014

5. NAME AT BIRTH OR OTHER NAME USED FOR PERSONAL BUSINESS

6a. AGE - Last Birthday	6b. UNDER 1 YEAR MONTHS / DAYS	6c. UNDER 1 DAY HOURS / MINUTES
30		

7a. LOCATION OF DEATH	7b. CITY, VILLAGE, OR TOWNSHIP OF DEATH	7c. COUNTY OF DEATH
27576 Willowood Drive 48045	Harrison Township	Macomb

8a. CURRENT RESIDENCE - STATE	8b. COUNTY	8c. LOCALITY	8d. STREET AND NUMBER
Michigan	Macomb	Harrison Township	27576 Willowood Drive

8e. ZIP CODE	9. BIRTHPLACE (City and State or Country)	10. SOCIAL SECURITY NUMBER	11. DECEDENT'S EDUCATION
48045	Alpena, Michigan	378 96 6347	Two Years College

12. RACE	13a. ANCESTRY	13b. HISPANIC ORIGIN	14. WAS DECEDENT EVER IN THE U.S. ARMED FORCES?
White	French / Norwegian	No	No

15. USUAL OCCUPATION	16. KIND OF BUSINESS OR INDUSTRY	17. MARITAL STATUS	18. NAME OF SURVIVING SPOUSE
Writer	Independent Writer	Never Married	n/a

19. FATHER'S NAME (First, Middle, Last)	20. MOTHER'S NAME BEFORE FIRST MARRIED (First, Middle, Last)
Thomas Jacobs	Jodi Vam

21a. INFORMANT'S NAME (Type/Print)	21b. RELATIONSHIP TO DECEDENT	21c. MAILING ADDRESS
Jodi Dale	Mother	38530 Town Hall Harrison Township, Michigan 48045

22. METHOD OF DISPOSITION	23a. PLACE OF DISPOSITION	23b. (City or Town, State)
Cremation	Irwin Cremation Service	Shelby Township, Michigan

24.	24b. LICENSE NUMBER	25. LICENSE NUMBER	26.
Robert Laban		5250	Wm. Sullivan Schwarzkopf Funeral Home, Inc. 233 Northbound Gratiot Avenue Mount Clemens, Michigan 48043-5745

27a. CERTIFIER	28a. ACTUAL OR PRESUMED TIME OF DEATH	28b. PRONOUNCED DEAD ON	28c. TIME PRONOUNCED DEAD
☑ Medical Examiner	Unknown	June 5, 2014	8:19 P M

29. MEDICAL EXAMINER CONTACTED?	30. PLACE OF DEATH	31. IF HOSPITAL
Yes	Home	n/a

27b. DATE SIGNED	27c. LICENSE NUMBER	32. MEDICAL EXAMINER'S CASE NUMBER	33. NAME OF ATTENDING PHYSICIAN IF OTHER THAN CERTIFIER
Chief Medical Examiner June 6, 2014	4301081020	0976/2014	n/a

34. NAME AND ADDRESS OF CERTIFYING PHYSICIAN
Daniel J. Spitz, M.D. 43585 Elizabeth Road Mt. Clemens, MI 48043

35a. REGISTRAR'S SIGNATURE	35b. DATE FILED
Carmella Sabaugh	JUN 09 2014

CAUSE OF DEATH		Approximate Interval Between Onset and Death
36. PART I.	Intoxication by Heroin	Unknown
IMMEDIATE CAUSE Pending Further Studies DUE TO (OR AS A CONSEQUENCE OF)		
a. Amended July 9, 2014 DUE TO (OR AS A CONSEQUENCE OF)		
b.		
c.		

PART II. OTHER SIGNIFICANT CONDITIONS	37. DID TOBACCO USE CONTRIBUTE TO DEATH?	38. IF FEMALE:
	☑ No	Not pregnant within past year

39. MANNER OF DEATH	40a. WAS AN AUTOPSY PERFORMED?	40b. WERE AUTOPSY FINDINGS AVAILABLE PRIOR TO COMPLETION OF CAUSE OF DEATH?
Accident	Yes	Yes

41a. DATE OF INJURY	41b. TIME OF INJURY	41c. DESCRIBE HOW INJURY OCCURRED
Unknown	Unknown	Drug abuse

42a. INJURY AT WORK	42b. PLACE OF INJURY	42c. IF TRANSPORTATION INJURY	42g. LOCATION
No	Home	N/A	27576 Willowood Dr., Harrison Twp., MI

Printed On 07-16-2014 at 11:09:35

Dane Jacobs

1983—2014

The little sailor on his first birthday

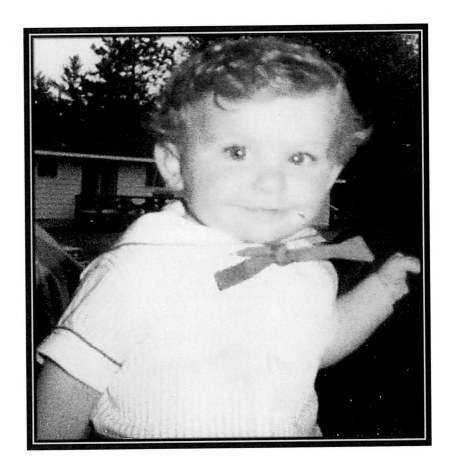

Little Swinger

Quinn's

Happy Mother's Day

Fun with Snakes in West Virginia

All Smiles on Vacation in West Virginia

The High School Rebel

Graduation Day

Kisses for Grandma

Dane's Hero--Grampa

Family Wedding

Joni &Lisa-Godmothers

Ray--Dane's Roommate at UDM

Them We Love Most—Family& Friends

Dane & Nicole

Close Friends Andy & Jeannie

Tim—Friend and Teacher

Even the Band Gets a Break

Best Friends Dane Mickey and Tony

Tigers Fans & Their Fat Heads

Decked Out—Ever Hopeful Detroit Lions Fans

BOOK 2

Dane-19 years old

We own a little beach house up north, in Forestville, Michigan where we all enjoyed spending time and leaving the busy city life behind. A short hour and 40-minute commute along the shoreline makes the small cottage very accessible to us—and when I say small, I mean small. The place is 440 square feet, with one bedroom. A pull out sofa allows two more people to sleep in relative comfort. A slightly larger wrap around deck provides an outdoor living space as well. We fondly refer to the place as "440 square feet of paradise." It sits squarely on our beachfront property and has a lovely sandy shore with a wonderful view of the shipping channel. We love to watch the freighters go by, as well as powerboats, yachts, and sailboats. Randy's brother Mark owns a similar place 100 feet from the north side of ours. The cottages have been in the family since the 1940's and with some remodels, were now very cozy little shacks.

A large bonfire pit and Tiki bar that resembles a Tijuana taxi sits in the middle and is shared by all. Randy, an avid fisherman, loves to spend long days on Lake Huron pursuing salmon, walleye, and bass. I prefer to park myself on the deck, sometimes in my hammock to nap and read. Dane loved the beach house. He and Mickey were frequent visitors. He also loved to read, bonfire, and laugh at Mickey's antics. He sometimes came up alone to play his guitar and write, reveling in the solitude he usually preferred. His love for the beach matched Randy's and mine. The place is simply a balm for our souls. But this weekend, Dane stayed in the city instead of joining us. We planned to leave early that day and meet him at home for dinner and laundry. I was still adjusting to him living at college and as usual, I missed him horribly. I would happily cook him his favorites, do his laundry, and catch up on our weeks' events. It would be a perfect ending to a perfect weekend.

That afternoon, as Randy and I were indulging in our favorite pastimes, my cell phone rang. I did not recognize the number on the screen, but answered it anyway. The man on the other end said that he owns a gas station in Detroit and that Dane had come into his store crawling on his hands and knees. He said Dane could barely speak as he told the man what my phone number was. Dane appeared very confused, so an ambulance was called and he was transported to Detroit Receiving Hospital. The kind owner said that Dane's truck could stay in his parking lot until we could come for it. I thanked him and immediately called Randy who was out fishing.

I could not imagine what the hell was going on. In a panic I realized that I may have to handle this by myself. Shaking like a leaf, I explained the sketchy details to him. Randy was a couple of miles offshore and it would take a while to pull the lines, run in, and trailer the boat and drive back to the cottage. I could not wait. I had my car up north, so I wouldn't have to wait for him to get back. He gave me directions down to the hospital and I was on the road in a few minutes. The drive from Forestville to Detroit is about two hours and fifteen minutes. I made the trip in under two hours. Somehow-and I can't remember how-I found the hospital.

Detroit Receiving is not in an area I was very familiar with. It's a gritty neighborhood which is made even more evident by the crazy confusion I was met with in the emergency room. Primarily a trauma hospital, D.R.H. is known for treating the indigent that are found in this and almost any inner city. I parked, grabbed my keys and purse and ran into the E.R. getting directions to Dane's bed, I walked down the hall. I found my son, pale as a ghost and hooked up to oxygen and other monitors.

He was awake and smiled dimly and gave me a weak wave. His "Hi Mom", gave me some small relief. "What happened?" I asked, after giving him a hug and a kiss. "I don't remember, Mom. I was driving home and suddenly everything went kind of black and I couldn't see. I got dizzy and had to pull over so I went into the gas station. I don't remember anything else."

Just then a doctor came in. He asked Dane if he had permission to share information with me. Dane allowed that it was okay. His blood test showed no hard drugs or alcohol in his system. The doctor said that by his vitals and levels, he thought that Dane had suffered a severe panic attack. "Has this ever happened before?" the doctor asked. Dane and I both shook our heads. Because he was stabilized, it was recommended that he be released and then follow up as soon as possible with our regular doctor. Years later, when I reminded Dane of this story, he had absolutely no recollection of it.

I drove Dane back to our house and got him comfortable. Randy arrived home and sat with Dane while he listened to the bizarre story. When we asked Dane what could have brought on such a severe panic attack, he said he wasn't sure. He had been feeling very stressed and overwhelmed lately. Things in his world seemed to be moving too fast and he didn't feel completely in control of his life anymore. Randy and I were puzzled. We had not noticed anything different in Dane's behavior.

Because he looked sleepy, I felt that the morning would be a better time to talk. This was our very first experience with his mental health issues. We had boarded the rollercoaster and the safety bar was tightly secured. It was beginning to pick up speed.

Dane slept in and when he finally stirred we discussed what was going on in his world. He had moved out of the dorms at the end of his first year at UDM and was living with two friends, Dave and Katrina, in Royal Oak Township. It was a very depressed area and Randy and I were not happy when he insisted moving in there. His neighbors scared me. Too many out of work people sitting idly around on porches doing nothing, drinking and smoking pot seemed to be the main activity. One such friend Dane made was a man called Papa. Papa was a shell shocked vet that slept in the back of a nearby abandoned pickup truck. Papa routinely came around to beg for cigarettes and money. If he was refused, sometimes he just rode off on his bike crying loudly. But Dane felt sorry for him and listened to his stories.

He loved the urban feel of his new home and was not threatened even a little bit. He got himself invited to neighborhood barbecues and made himself at quite at home with his neighbors. But when I called him, more and more it seemed like he was having a hard time. Although he loved and respected his roomies, other factors made it apparent that the situation was proving to be too stressful for him. I worried that he didn't have the necessary coping skills to share a home.

Because we didn't know what else to do, Randy and I decided that it would be best if he would move back home, get some medical attention, and relax a little. It was settled and within a day or two, Dane was home and all set up in his old room. We made an appointment with our family doctor and he suggested a therapist that possibly could help him.

He was also prescribed his very first dose of anti-depressants—the first of many that we would try. They found a psychiatrist within our insurance plan and Dane was set up to see her three times a week. Our insurance would cover the therapy at fifty percent and we would have to pick up the rest of the fee. He liked talking to her and we all thought that it seemed to help him. Although Dane and I always shared things, I was flummoxed on the right words to say to comfort him. It was easier for him to speak honestly with her.

After the incident in the gas station he was given his first medication and therapy where the first of many doctors diagnosed Dane with depression and severe anxiety. The first time he took a prescribed medication for his diagnosis, was the official start of a 12-year battle with mental illness. His diagnosis would change with every doctor, every hospitalization and every incident. Dane saw so many doctors and therapists over the course of this horrible war, I've lost count. He was prescribed every psychotropic drug on the menu at one time or another and diagnosed with every mental illness imaginable by the mental health professionals.

We read up an attempt to educate ourselves on these issues and tried to be aware of how we could help him. It was a fight with no relief in sight. The human brain is still not well understood and it seems to be able to outsmart everything everyone trying to help, tried. Over the next few years, Dane would have breakdowns and suicide attempts that put him in every mental hospital in the area. We fought our fight with insurance companies to get the coverage needed to assist in this venture. Randy was the most supportive and generous stepfather Dane could have ever asked for. He selflessly gave whatever time and money it took to ease Dane's pain and assist in his care. And Dane and I both love him for it.

I don't want to get into all of the details of bi-polar, depression, paranoia, severe anxiety and every other medical term. It would be a whole another book just to write the list. I have to explain it though, because mental illness and eventual drug addiction go hand in hand; the frustration of treating mental conditions which most often leads to self-medicating. It's a one-two punch that is nearly impossible to recover from-even with all the love and support we could give him.

Dane-20 years old

One night, in 2003, I was lying in bed reading. Dane appeared at my bedside looking pale and very sad. "What's up, babe?" Realizing that he had tears streaming down his face, I put my book down and asked him, "What's wrong? Are you okay?" Dane came over to Randy's side of the bed and stretched out beside me. "I don't know what to do, Mom. I don't want to live anymore. It's too hard and I don't know if I can go on." My blood ran icy cold. With a sick heart and false calm, I asked him what he thought we should do. He could barely catch his breath. I was the first to speak. "Okay, we're going to the hospital. I'm sure they will know how to help."

I persuaded Dane to get up and together we walked downstairs to get Randy. One look at Dane's face, and Randy jumped up and took his arm. I told my husband that we had an emergency and we would all need to go to St. John's hospital. Two minutes later we were out the door and in the truck. In a small voice, Dane asked me if I minded sitting in the back seat with him. I unstrapped and moved to the backseat where I held a shaking and crying Dane all the way there.

Upon arriving at the E.R., Dane was evaluated. They interviewed him and asked many questions. We had not yet learned the way to handle getting him actually admitted for mental health care. All Dane would say was that he was very sad and tired of living. The nurse took notes and presently he was moved to a bed.

He was given Ativan to relax him. Soon, it was determined that he was stable and not a threat to himself or others. We were advised to find him a psychologist as soon as possible, and Dane was released. I was infuriated and felt that our situation was not taken seriously. We had no idea what to do, or how to handle this new development. Losing the will to live would be a recurring theme from this day forward.

I had only cracked the spine on the book of mental hospital protocol and was only beginning to study the lessons. I still had very much to learn. We waited while Dane was officially released and quietly we drove home. Dane slept through the night without further incident.

We spent the next week learning some navigational skills regarding mental health care and insurance. Had we been able to admit Dane, the treatment would have been covered by our policy at fifty percent. However, we now would have to search for a psychiatrist that even accepted our insurance and hope for the best.

It was advised that our family doctor would not be qualified to diagnose his condition. Dane ended up seeing his new doctor several times and still he was officially undiagnosed.

Meds would be given and changed in an effort to figure out exactly what he was suffering from. The whole process was just fire and miss. Trial and mostly error, Dane, as well as us, became completely frustrated. "Mom, I feel like a fuckin' guinea pig!"

I cannot think of an anti-depressant or anxiety med that we did not try. The pills du jour would take about a month to take full effect. Maybe they would work for a while before the side effects would hit. And he just became sadder. Sometimes the side effects were as bad as the disease. Maybe he would gain weight fast-a condition he hated. Or got real skinny and pale. Miserably he would slog around the house doing the "Thorazine shuffle", until I couldn't watch it any longer.

Back to the doctor we would go, demanding to try something else. His mouth would get dry and he would drink water constantly. One med would not let him urinate and force him to spend hours in the bathroom frustrated just trying to pee. He constantly had the shakes. Upset stomach and diarrhea added to his discomfort. Restless leg syndrome was another side effect that made him feel like bugs were crawling under his skin. Luckily, he was prescribed a med that eliminated that misery. His sleep pattern got mixed up and he was unable to sleep at night, napping on and off all day. He either ate everything in sight or gagged down just enough food to stay alive. It was a horrid experience to watch him go through.

He was absolutely miserable but was trying to remain hopeful as the doctors guessed, guessed, and then guessed again at a diagnosis.

This time period was our first understanding of how very futile psychotropic drugs can be. We later would even consider electro shock therapy. We read up on it but Dane was scared to possibly lose his short term memory. He felt that with an unsure future, his memories may be all that he was left with. I now wish we would have tried it. Maybe it would have been the one thing that worked. Nothing excited him and even moments of happiness were fleeting. He would restlessly watch movies and listen to his music trying to engage normally. He simply lost interest in the very things he always loved, and was unable to sustain any sort of joy.

Pills

The white ones get me out of bed

These little blue deals are daytime help.

Take two before I leave for work

And red and blue together at half till ten

My insurance is the best

Doctors nowadays are so smart

To feel will be an action of past

In my current state all that I can say

Is that maybe it's the best way.

I'll always have memories

Random frames in times

With no emotion attached.

So surprising when it's gone

And you've signed to see it go

A few sad notions, a wince of pain

Worth running from and

hiding under cotton

Eat and extra one for this or that

till it's just another in your hand.

©Dane Jacobs

Dane-21 years old

After two years, sadly, Dane dropped out of college. For the rest of his life, he hated the fact that he had failed at his long time goal. It was very embarrassing to him that all of his friends finished college and went on to enjoy careers. But Dane still was their best cheerleader and was very proud of all of his friend's successes. He just couldn't handle the pressure that he put on himself and made it impossible to continue his education. He was petrified of failure and seemed to just give up rather than soldier on. It was decided that he would go back to work at O.L. Johnson full time with Randy until he and we could figure things out.

That was all well and fine for a while. I knew Dane was smoking pot and now that he was 21, legally drinking. I relaxed a little about the pot. It seemed to help his anxiety more than his prescription for Xanax which, in his words, made him "feel strange." I wasn't concerned with the few beers he shared with the guys after work. Never once, save for a time up north when he drank some shots, had I ever seen him drunk.

Later I learned that there had been plenty of times, I just hadn't seen it. I thought I knew the "high" look, but that was not even apparent anymore; he was usually drugged with prescribed medications. He seemed under control to our naïve eyes. Up until now, Dane had never given us reason to doubt his judgement. He was still seeing his therapist and doctor regularly. Sometimes moody, Dane was having trouble working 40 hours a week. Randy let him cut back his hours, allowing him to work just on the days he felt strong enough. Hopefully, that plan would reduce some of his stress. We considered it more important to work on his health.

I felt frustrated at this time and wondered if Dane was trying hard enough. I thought the meds would be more helpful. He seemed to be sleeping more and more and the moods were starting to swing faster. I was beginning to recognize a distinct pattern of highs and lows. Soon he was diagnosed with bipolar mood disorder. He was sometimes sluggish and I wondered again if he was smoking too much pot. He assured me that it was the same as always, and again, I believed him.

During this time, his friends seemed to drop off, and I couldn't blame them. Dane was a very unreliable person and certainly not easy to be friends with. I do remember a girl named Nicole who was very sweet to him. One time she brought him a cake and he declared that it was the best cake he had ever eaten.

She was very compassionate and listened to him tell her how he was feeling. But you just could never count on him. He would say that he would be somewhere at a certain time and then just not show up at all. And not even bother to call to explain. He was becoming more and more detached from things and isolating himself further. He would attend an occasional party or concert, but not often. He spent the majority of his time off work at home watching movies, reading, and sleeping.

I was confounded as what to do to help him. Randy and I included him in whatever we were doing and he still loved going up North with us. He also went to Ossineke to visit his old friends and our family. I later learned that the parties up north included drugs and alcohol. The numerous hunting camps and cottages in secluded areas made partying easy.

I never realized anything abnormal was going on when we were "home" in Ossineke.

When I was 18, it was legal to drink and we certainly did our share. Deciding how much freedom to give your child is very hard to figure out, especially when they become of legal age. Our best hope is that they use some reasonable judgement during these times, but peer pressure will always trump Mom and Dad pressure.

Shock

A wandering eye

sweeping the distance

from land to sky.

And at this instant

floored by shock at what I've found

A lustre shines

divine.

Is it enough to guide me?

Bright enough to see through

Something beside me.

©Dane Jacobs

I also read this silly observation:

long hair = getting laid

Dane-22 years old

While Dane was still living with us, we had him in therapy and his doctor was still working on medication to stabilize him. We thought we were dealing with anxiety and depression and that's what his medicines were supposed to address. During this time another symptom reared its' ugly head—mania.

When in a manic state, Dane would appear sweaty and chatter non-stop, dominating all conversations. He would be totally restless, hopping up from his chair and pacing around during these animated, gesticulated stories. He would follow me around the house talking about various and unrelated subjects at a wild speed. He mostly was able to still work and during these times he ripped through his job doing things at breakneck pace. He had money to spend and we quickly learned that he had to be monitored if at all possible. A lover of thrift stores, Dane would hit up a Salvation Army and spend 200.00 or more on clothes as well as things he didn't really need. Yes, I agreed that they were wonderful deals, but he simply did not need that many clothes. On one haul, he proudly showed me 10 pairs of blue jeans and about 20 shirts and tee shirts. He also had a pile of books. He was so excited to wash everything and start wearing his newfound treasures. Jeannie, our beloved secretary, would also be an audience to his fashion shows. She patiently listened and watched his little show and tells as he held up each item and told her of the incredibly good deals that he had stumbled upon. Jeannie would nod and agree that he was a fabulous shopper.

One June weekend Randy and I were at the cottage while Dane chose to relax at home. It was Father's Day weekend and we would leave early on Sunday so we could all have dinner together to honor Poppy. Dane called us earlier in the day to remind us of our dinner date and to say that he had a surprise for Pops. I couldn't imagine what he had up his sleeve. Upon arriving home later that afternoon, I instantly recognized the telltale signs of mania. Dane greeted us at the door. Sweaty and with wide eyes he called out, "Happy Father's Day Poppy! Hurry up, I've got something to show you! C'mon downstairs!" So, we all trouped down to the basement. Again, I could not imagine what this gift was going to be. The smell of Pine Sol hit me immediately. Stunned, we slowly looked around to take this all in. The basement absolutely sparkled. We have two 8 feet long by 2 feet wide by 8 feet high shelves that hold various decorations, miscellaneous tax info, Randy's hunting clothes and other random tubs of stuff. The shelves appeared perfectly organized. He told us that he had been up all night cleaning. He took everything off of the shelves and scrubbed them down. He then put everything in large Rubbermaid tubs and labeled them accordingly. The floor had been vacuumed and mopped. The area of his bedroom was completely pristine. Randy and I were simply amazed and slack jawed as we surveyed his handiwork. This was a task that we had been procrastinating for months. Even so, I don't know if Randy and I could have made it look this good.

Dane explained how he got the idea that this project would be a great gift for Randy for Father's Day. He started the job on Saturday afternoon and worked through the night to finish it by morning. He then asked us what we were doing for dinner because he was getting a little tired.

We were able to get the mania part of his bipolar under control somewhat, but there were still times he would clean with a toothbrush and obsessively organize his things. He even concocted his own cleaning potions that he was convinced were superior. Books, albums and his closet would in perfect order and his living area would be spotless.

One afternoon, while Dane was in high school, he came in carrying a guitar. Curiously, I asked, "where did you get that thing?" He explained that it was a friend's, and he was borrowing it. "Come watch me, Mom. I can play a little!" He proceeded to kick out a little jam for me. Almost any other person and I may have been surprised that he could play. I had no idea, and I think he surprised himself, that he was a natural musician. As a grade school child, I remember that the school gave musical aptitude tests. Dane scored very high and the music teacher suggested that he choose an instrument and take lessons. But even at 10 he thought with his school work and sports, he didn't have the time. Grades always came first for Dane.

Music lessons were simply a commitment he wasn't ready to take on. I have to say, I was disappointed with his choice. But on that day, he was strumming out a tune. For hours he would practice and developed a little slap style that would eventually become his signature. We ended up buying the guitar from his friend—the first of many guitars to come. I loved hearing the sounds of his music floating up the stairs. Often he would have me come down to hear a riff that he was working on. "Which one sounds better, Mom?" he would ask. With persistence, he taught himself to play. A few years later, my friend Tim was over for a visit. Tim is my yoga instructor, and we forged a strong friendship as we practiced and studied yoga theories. A modern day true renaissance man, Tim sings, paints, acts, writes, and plays music.

He creates tunes and has a lengthy musical history involving numerous bands. A showman on stage, everybody in the audience is drawn to him. He is the best yoga teacher I have ever practiced with. His calming bass voice is very soothing as he coaxes the knots out of our bodies, and helps us to clear our minds. On that day, Dane happened to be beatin' on his guitar. I called down to the basement for Dane to come up and show Tim what he was working on.

Tim and I ended up going downstairs to his room where Dane, shyly, played a little for us. When he finished his solo, Tim looked at me and said, "Mama, your boy can play." Well, the smile that crossed Dane's face was epic-only to be matched by mine! With that, an impromptu jam session took place. My niece, Nicole was spending a few days with us and could be found sitting on Dane's bed, listening. Tim suggested that they write a song together. "What should we write about, Nicole? What's your favorite thing to do?" "Well, I love to shop and then go to Starbucks" was her reply. With Dane on bass and Nicole smiling wildly, Tim adlibbed and created a little tune. The rest is history. Soon Dane and Tim were regularly practicing together. Tim decided that the two of them should create some songs and do a little coffee house tour. When Dane agreed, I was ecstatic that he was finally going to pursue music and isolate less.

They worked tirelessly writing and playing original songs and I loved it. I was born to be a 'Band Mom' and could be counted on to listen as well as provide snacks and drinks. All of this happened shortly after Dane's first mental health stay and he was still slightly fragile. I seriously doubted his ability to go on a stage and perform. It would not be unusual for him to get a panic attack and be too nervous to do the show. We would just have to cross our fingers and hope for the best. The first gig was scheduled to take place in Grosse Pointe Park at Cuppacino coffee house. A few days prior, Dane expressed to Randy that he didn't have anything to wear for his first performance. Dane has always respected Randy's taste in clothing. A bit of a clotheshorse and an avid shopper, Randy's vast closet was always fair game for Dane to borrow from. But this time was different. For this special occasion, the two of them happily skipped off to the mall to find him some new threads.

Hours later, after Dane conned Randy out of a steak dinner, they showed up at home carrying numerous shopping bags. The pants and shirts purchased would cover this gig as well as a few others. Proudly, Dane modeled what he thought what he would wear to the show. And they nailed it. He looked perfect.

As the date approached, we invited many friends to come out and support Dane and Tim on their maiden show. Uncles Mark and Marty came over for the weekend and I was so happy to have them be a part of this important event. We got there early and got our table front and center. I was so nervous waiting for them to take the stage.

After they were announced, Tim and Dane walked out and took their places. Dane sat on a stool in front of a red and black graphically painted wall. With a serious look on his face, he picked up his bass and played through the eight songs they had been rehearsing. With great relief, I sighed. We clapped and cheered wildly and Dane smiled shyly. On their break, a few girls came to our table and asked me if I was the bass players Mom. Well, yes, I said proudly, I am. They asked me if Dane had a girlfriend. My God, I thought, he had fans! I told them that was a question for Dane to answer. They ended up cornering him after the show and a happy Dane experienced his first taste of 'band groupies'. I was insanely proud and happy for him.

The band thing went on for a while even after Dane had moved to Grosse Pointe Park. Practices were held at his apartment, probably much to the chagrin of the other house dwellers.

But I was seeing cracks in the armor as Dane sometimes didn't feel like rehearsing. It was becoming more of a struggle than a pleasure. But he forged on for a while, and they expanded by adding two gorgeous biracial girl singers to the band. Their lovely voices as well as their beauty added to the show as they sang and danced on the stage. Dane loved his 'little sistas!' With Tim being black and the girls of mixed color, Dane stood out. Play that funky music white boy!

On a visit back home one day, Dane ran up to Pete's Party Store, a close half a mile from our home. He needed a Pepsi and M&M's, he left and said he'd be right back. A bit later a very excited Dane returned with his goodies in hand and explained how he had run into a girl from high school. He happened to be putting up a flyer advertising his latest gig and she tapped him on the shoulder. She told him that she had a bit part in a movie and was hoping to be an actress. Dane assured her that she was too pretty for that nonsense. He gave her details about the show and she promised to try to make it out for the event. They hugged and promised to stay in touch. Heading down to his room, Dane grabbed his bass and began writing a song about her. He and Tim put the final touches on it and "You're Too Pretty for Pictures" became one of my favorites.

After recording a c.d. and playing Cuppacino as well as many art fairs, the band eventually fizzled out. As much as he loved playing, Dane could not be counted on to be a full participant. All in all, the band experience was very good for him, his skill at music was constantly improving. Around this time, he began collecting vinyl albums. He haunted the used music stores as well as thrift stores and garage sales as his collection grew. His Grampa built him a stand that held his collection. He loved the classic rock album covers and admonished me for selling all my albums before moving in with Randy. He acquired an old turntable and we found it a new needle. We spent long hours listening and debating the audio differences in L.P.s and C.D. s. Once at a farmer's market in Port Austin, Dane found the album containing the soundtrack from Midnight Cowboy-a movie he loved. He was beyond excited at unearthing this treasure. Sadly, I thought that he identified with the track by Harry Nilsson. "Everybody's talking at me", was Dane, over and over.

"Everybody's talking at me.

I don't hear a word they're saying,

Only the echoes of my mind.

People stopping staring,

I can't see their faces,

Only the shadows of their eyes.

I'm going where the sun keeps shining

Thru' the pouring rain,

Going where the weather suits my clothes,

Backing off the North East wind,

Sailing on a summer breeze

And skipping over the ocean like a stone."
© **Fred Neil**

I promised all of his albums to his buddy Tony who has many memories of the times they shared listening to them. But not 'Midnight Cowboy'. That one is mine and I will forever remember his delight at finding it.

Dane was always trying to expand Randy and my musical taste, while I was doing the same thing for him. We both have an affinity for old southern rock and he turned me on to early rap. He loved the Beastie Boys and was amused that I saw the boys live in 1985 when they opened for Madonna. I didn't care for them then, but later developed a taste for 'Intergalactic.' Dane and I had this thing where if ever we were anywhere and Intergalactic came on the radio, we would immediately call each other. Silly, I know, but just one of the things we did. I could be half asleep when the call would come in and I would hear that unmistakable heavy bass. "Intergalactic, Mom. Talk to you later. I love you." I would smile and go to sleep. I have an old Beastie Boys t-shirt that I sometimes wear when I want to feel close to him. We knew every word to 'Gin and Juice' and 'Regulate" and loved to rap along. He could do an amazing imitation of Snoop Dogg and would get me giggling uncontrollably every time. On the other side of the musical spectrum, we both loved James Taylor and would spend long hours at the beach house quietly reading with sweet baby James on in the background

It wasn't long before Dane felt he was strong enough to move back out on his own. He found an apartment in Grosse Pointe Park that met our approval and he and his college buddy, Tony moved in. I loved when he lived there. The place was an old house divided up into three apartments and their space was on the first floor in the front. There was a small yard and a porch they could enjoy. The neighborhood was quite eclectic with young couples as well as retirees making their home on Wayburn Street. I used to call it "Wayburn for the wayward," and the boys would laugh. Wayburn is located just off Kercheval in an area of Grosse Pointe Park known as 'the cabbage patch' and I hoped our cute little cabbage patch kids would grow and be happy there. It was a short two block walk to the funky little downtown area. He often shopped at the local hardware that was featured in the Clint Eastwood movie called 'Gran Torino'. Dane loved to hit Cuppacino as well as Janet's Lunch. Janet's restaurant sat about ten people at a small bar area and served the very best blueberry pancakes I have ever tasted. As semi-regulars, the cooks would smile and wave as they saw us take a stool at the counter. Dane proudly made me watch as they mixed up the batter from scratch. We spent many Saturday mornings drinking coffee and feasting on these yummy treats.

It was during this time that the depression seemed to quietly sneak back in; worse than ever. Dane was once again having trouble making it into work and would hole up and not answer his phone for days. I would get so worried and inevitably end up driving to Grosse Point Park to check on him. The short drive would take me 15 minutes if I hurried. I would find him on the couch, looking horribly despaired with big tears sliding down his face. "I just can't do it, Mom. It's all such a struggle. What's the matter with me?"

We would schedule another doctor appointment and Dane would begin the process of weaning off of one anti-depressant and starting a new one. Sometimes, he'd bounce back a little and things would even out a bit. He would force himself to go back to work. But it got worse. He started missing too many days. He said the guys at work were getting under his skin. Dane was of the opinion that nobody was working hard enough; a fact that was ironic considering how much work he was missing. He felt a loyalty to Randy and couldn't stand anyone feeling otherwise. He thought everyone was looking at him and talking about him. It bothered him so much that he would put himself into a funk and spiral back down. Of course, this affected us all. Randy and I spent many frustrating hours at Dane's trying to reason with him and talk him down from the ledge, while poor Jeannie was stuck picking up his slack at work. It was a very helpless feeling for all of us.

It was also hard to ignore the fact that Dane seemed high more and more. He didn't bother to hide his pot and left it out in plain sight. A little window ledge garden held some plants and a giant water pipe was the centerpiece of his coffee table. "Isn't it cool, Mom? The colored glass makes it look like a piece of art!" He looked horrible and had grown a beard. With constant red eyes and a disheveled look, everybody was noticing the changes in Dane and becoming concerned. He was getting more and more into his isolation and we needed to understand the relationship between his meds and his street drugs. He argued that it was two separate things, but nonetheless things were getting worse.

It was during this time that Mickey came into Dane's life. Or maybe Dane came into his. It was the classic question of 'who rescued who?' Always the animal lover, Dane had his eye on two puppies that could be found hanging around work. He saw the two of them patrolling the corner party store in search of any scraps they could forage, snacking on chicken bones and pizza crusts. It was very evident that they were not fed or cared for-a situation that enraged Dane.

One morning while driving to work he spotted the female puppy lying dead on the side of the street. Moved to tears, he resolved to save the little male. When the pup came into the parking lot at work, Dane would scoop him up in his arms and walk him back to the house that owned the dog. He saw that the puppy was living in a dirt floor garage on a chain he could easily slip out of. There was no food or water in sight. Sadly, Dane put him back on the chain. The next day, again on his way to work, Dane witnessed cars screeching to a halt as the dog was running loose in the morning traffic. That did it, for Dane. He pulled his truck over, opened his door, and called the puppy. The dog simply jumped into Dane's truck where he curled up on the seat and slept all day. Dane headed into the office and had Randy come out to meet his new grand dog. The two of them then called me on Randy's cell to describe the dog. Dane said that he was maybe three months old, kind of reddish in color with a black five o'clock shadow. Randy said, "He's really cute and you are going to love him." Later that summer, one afternoon while Mickey was at work with Dane, a child on the other side of the fence spotted him. She pointed her small finger at him and said, "dat look like DeShawn!" Mickey didn't even turn around. He ducked back inside the warehouse and he never looked back.

Dane was out of his mind excited with his little rescue. After work, he drove to a pet store and bought him a collar, leash, food dishes, toys and food. When I called him that night, I was curious as to what he named the dog. "Mom, since I found him at the corner of McNichols and Conant, I'm going to name him McNichols F. Conant. But we'll just call him 'Mickey'. "What's the 'F' for?" I asked. "It's subjective. We'll just fill it in with what is appropriate at the time!" Okay, that works. Over the years I heard poor Mick's middle name be "Freebird", "Freeballs", and "Fucktard" and others equally as colorful. The fact that the landlord did not allow pets could be a problem but Dane taught Mickey to bark only in case of emergency. Mickey's tenure at "Wayburn for the wayward" went unnoticed.

Mickey was the best thing that ever happened to Dane. It gave him something to love. And we lovingly called him the "ghetto terrier." With Detroit having an average of one pit bull to every three residents, there was a good chance that the Mickster was part pit bull. He usually cocked his head to the side with one ear up and one ear down, giving him a perpetually quizzical look. He was a sweet dog and I loved the fact that Dane had something to care for and keep him grounded. He proudly walked Mickey around the neighborhood and Tony included him in his long runs around Grosse Pointe. Most days he went to work with Dane and was coined the official 'Strut Mutt'.

With strut being our main steel product, the handle was a total crack up. With his red bandana on, Mickey endeared himself to everyone he met. My brother claims that to this day, Mick still has wax under his toenails from when he scratched the winning lottery ticket. Nobody can argue that!

In 2003 Randy's brother Mark finally proposed to longtime girlfriend, Cheryl and a wedding was planned to be held up north with the reception to be celebrated right on our beach property. Cheryl had seemed like a family member for years, and we already loved her like a sister. Dane was particularly fond of Aunt Cheryl and she was the recipient of many of his bear hugs. She always gave him her attention and was always interested in him. As the details were finalized for a July 2004 wedding, Randy had the idea that in addition to the regular band we had scheduled, maybe Dane and Tim could play as the warm up. The boys agreed and practiced their old tunes. The day of the wedding dawned sunny and gorgeous as we rushed around perfecting the tables, flowers and decorations. Just in the nick of time for the ceremony, Dane, Tim and Mickey rolled down the hill to the cottage. I was disappointed to see Dane dressed in torn jeans, a raggedy t-shirt and a dirty baseball hat. He was also in a rather crabby mood and was very touchy when I commented on his look. I had the sinking feeling that this was not going to be a good day.

After the ceremony, we proceeded back to the beach for the reception. The yard filled with friends and family getting cocktails and enjoying the view. We had a fabulous barbecue dinner and soon it was time for Tim and Dane to start playing. But no one had seen Dane in a while. I frantically searched the crowd looking for him. I checked his truck and in the cottage but found no sign of him.

Two of our friends jumped on our four wheelers and went off down the beach in search. A bit later they came back with Dane on the back of one of the bikes. He was pale as a ghost. Our friends Shawn and Benny said that they found him about a quarter of a mile down the beach, sitting in his underwear in the water along the shore. He was confused but they were able to persuade him to dress and come back to the party. I was shaken at this story and had Dane join me in the cottage. He said he felt helpless and scared. There were too many people looking at him. I asked that he just not let Uncle Mark and Aunt Cheryl (who he adored) down. "Just play your songs and then you can relax," I told him.

Finally, Dane and Tim took the stage. They got through their tunes but it was very obvious that Dane's heart was just not in it. The boys were supposed to spend the night with us where they could freely drink without having to worry about driving back to the city. But that wasn't meant to be as Dane explained that all the people were making him very nervous.

He wanted to be at his apartment in his quiet and familiar environment. I was torn between doing my bridesmaid duties and enjoying the party we had planned or going home to care for a very depressed Dane. He begged me to stay and Tim said he would take care of Dane. Reluctantly, I hugged him and made him promise to call me later.

He did call me about two hours later and sounded much better and more relieved. He and Mickey were watching a movie. I slapped on a happy face and got through the night.

Later when I tried to discuss this with Dane, once again, he had absolutely no recollection of this event. He doubted what I was saying and I reminded him that he could ask Tim, Shawn, or Benny for the facts. He was too embarrassed to do that and decided to take my word for it. With tears running down his face Dane said that he was getting very scared and he was losing control of his life. I immediately scheduled another doctor appointment for some further evaluation. I was petrified that this roller coaster was gaining speed and taking wild turns.

Dane-age 23-24

Within a year or so, Tony got accepted into a law college and had plans to move out of the Grosse Pointe Park apartment. Dane was unable to afford it alone and the search began for a cheaper place to live. He found a darling studio apartment in Detroit at the Parkhurst Apartments that was pet friendly and would accept Mickey as a resident. The West Village of Detroit hosts a number of large apartment buildings and gorgeous old mansions. We learned that Jack White of the White Stripes lived in Indian Village, just two blocks away. On a very bitter cold December night, we moved him in. The apartment building was huge and Dane's view on the seventh floor was of Belle Isle. The place had a 24-hour guard posted outside as well as an old fashioned desk with an attendant where Dane would pick up his mail. The entrance was grand and had a large foyer with gleaming hardwood floors, a fireplace and a piano. Tapestry style rugs and antiques with art work added to the elegant feel. His apartment had the same shining floors and was freshly painted throughout. A team of maintenance men kept the place spiffy and clean.

Dane quickly made friends with all of the staff and as usual, Mickey endeared himself to everyone. We all laughed as Mickey would walk into the elevator and watch the floor numbers go up to seven. As if he had done it all his life, Mick would know to step off and turn right, stopping outside the door to his new home. Dane was very content in the new place and loved chatting up the girls that worked at the front desk. But I had misgivings about him living 30 minutes from us. His health would be even harder to monitor at that distance. But the price was right and it was a quick commute to work for him. And Dane always enjoyed living in an urban setting. "Cross your fingers," I thought to myself.

Then the bottom fell out of our world. Randy had been managing O.L. Johnson for 23 years and plans were in place for him to buy out the owner and make the company officially ours. Randy had solely run the place and built up the business with his blood, sweat and tears. He was completely dedicated to the company and its employees. In May, new owners walked in and announced that Randy no longer would be working there. Unbelievably, Randy and Dane were fired and escorted off the property like common criminals. In utter shock, Randy called me and told me the news; those bastards.

That very afternoon, Randy got working on plans to open his own business—a goal that he had always had in the back of his mind. The dream was taking place faster and more urgently that he could have imagined. One of the repercussions of this was that once again, Dane would be unable to make his rent. There was no way he could stay in Detroit in that cool apartment with no income. Reluctantly, he moved home again

It was a flurry of activity when for the next three months there were giant white boards on the walls of our house with lists of things to do and goals for the new company. It was decided that we would name the company after my husband, with an orange and silver logo featuring a giant hard hat. 99% of our employees left OL Johnson with Randy. I loved that the majority of our new employees defected and joined us at the new company, loyalty is earned.

For weeks I hosted a think tank like atmosphere as things fell into place. Our kitchen bar was crowded and noisy as plans fell into place. Dane was on his computer entering part numbers for weeks. What a crazy time it was as a building was located and leased, equipment purchased, delivery trucks leased, computers and phones installed, as well as product, furniture, office space and supplies were put into place. With our long time secretary, Jeannie, in place, on August 01, 2007, we opened our doors and began doing business. Randy and Dane's firing turned out to be a blessing in disguise and the best thing we've ever done. Randy and his 'baby' are doing well to this day.

However, Dane was struggling and anxious about the change. After his move home and being instrumental at helping set up the computers for the new company, he broke down once again. He came into our bedroom one night and confessed that he didn't think he could go on. He simply did not care to live. He doubted he could properly do his job. His depression was once again in control of his thoughts. We all were in tears as we piled into Randy's truck. In five minutes we were heading down I-94 on our way to St. John's Hospital to get the inpatient mental health care he needed. In his interview, when asked if he thought he would harm himself or others, Dane answered, "Yes." It was all they needed to hear to admit him once again.

It was then that we learned a very important lesson in mental health hospitalizations. It is absolutely imperative that these exact words be said. **You must say that you will harm someone else or yourself. Exactly that**. They are the magic words that "open sesame" the doors to get some immediate therapy.

Dane was there a week and then transferred to another facility for two more weeks. He did the work and was getting stronger. Soon he was ready to come home and start his new job as our accounts receivable manager. We were all cautiously optimistic.

It was like old home week as Dane moved into his desk next to Jeannie. The dynamic duo was once again in place answering the phones and taking care of accounts. Dane handled the receivables and Jeannie will tell you that to this day, no one did the job faster and more accurately than Dane did. I bought him a cool bamboo plant for his desk and he added a framed picture of Mickey. And once again, we hoped for the best.

Things went pretty well for a while, before the old demons settled on his shoulders once again. Dane thought everyone was making fun of him and talking behind his back. He was sure that they were laughing at him. I reminded him that these co-workers had worked with him since he was 14 years old and cared very much about him. Jeannie was helpful as she lovingly listened and tried to reassure him. He was convinced someone was, "fucking with his stuff." He worked himself up so much that somedays he could not walk into the building. He would call Randy from the parking lot and Randy would go out to talk to him. Dane would be sitting in his car, pale and sweating. Randy would sometimes be able to convince him to come in and work and other times he had to send him home. It became clear that the perceived stress was just too much for him. His anxiety was getting worse and the medication was only marginally at best helping. Sadly, we put him on a part time schedule and upped his therapy appointments.

The rollercoaster was moving now, picking up some real speed.

Randy and I skipped our annual August vacation in the Keys that year because of the business just being too new. Dane's health was too fragile for me to be comfortable being away from him anyway. We did manage to get away in March for a much needed vacation. With cell phones, computers and fax machines, Randy could work from the condo. It's never the same as actually being on site, but it gave him enough control that he could have the best of both worlds. Dane stayed back home and we spoke many times a day. He kept up with his therapy appointments, but I was still anxious to get back home to make sure that he was okay.

I was always nervous anytime we were apart. Seeing him suffer through depression and anxiety was very hard for me to do, It simply crushed me to see him struggle so hard and have such minimal success. I have depression issues also, but I am one of the lucky ones. By that I mean, I was diagnosed, and prescribed an anti-depressant to treat my condition. It took a few tries, but we eventually found the right one. The medicine keeps me from bottoming out. I feel in control of my condition.

Dane-25 years old

Happily, the July 04, 2008 weekend was upon us. Being our favorite holiday, we were looking forward to our usual shenanigans. Traditionally Randy, Dane and I would head up to the beach house for the long weekend. Mark and Cheryl and children J.D., Matt, and Nicole would be in their cottage right next door. We would have a family centered weekend doing the things that made us happy. We all loved to enjoy the beach holidays that included bonfires, s'mores, cookouts and stargazing. Dane loved astronomy and could easily point out the location of the constellations. It was not unusual for many neighbor friends to drop in and have a beer or two with us at our tiki bar-that was always open. The bar's colorful, tropical decor and bright twinkle lights was like a beacon that we were all drawn to. The stereo system Mark set up provided us all the Jimmy Buffet tunes we needed to make the scene complete. On that holiday, the weather report promised a perfect forecast for fun and family bonding. Dane loved seeing his cousins and had a special connection with his cousin, Nicole. At just a few years younger, Nicole and Dane laughed at their many private inside jokes and had a blast driving around in my Mustang convertible with the stereo blasting.

But something seemed off that weekend. Dane was moody and quiet. He stayed inside reading or watching movies on his computer. He had no interest in joining us on the boat. I coaxed him out to the bonfire where he sat for a while, unengaged in the conversation. Shortly after, he went back inside to read. I gave him a few minutes to settle in and then went to check on him. With quiet tears, he explained that he just didn't feel comfortable. Like he didn't fit it. It killed my heart a little to see him fight so hard to be a part of things that came normal for everyone else. I asked him how I could help. "I want to go home." I wasn't surprised- just very disappointed. We decided that tomorrow morning, if he still felt the same way he could leave. In the morning, Dane packed up his things and Mickey and he drove back to the city. He agreed to call me as soon as he got back home. A few hours later Dane called to say that he made it home safely but forgot to get a house key or the garage remote and could not get into the house. Oh, brother. I had meant to but had forgotten to hide an extra key outside. I wasn't about to drive a three-and-a-half-hour round trip to let him in. It was decided that he would just camp out at a nearby hotel until tomorrow when we would be coming home anyway. He called again later, from his hotel bed to say that he and Mickey were safe and comfortable. He had ordered a pizza and was going to watch a movie and get some rest. "I'm fine Mom. Have fun and don't worry. I'll see you tomorrow. I love you." "I love you, too."

It turned out that this event was the first of many lies that I would fall for as Dane figured out what to say to make me feel secure and not worry so much. I later learned, because he finally confessed, that this was the starting point of his escape into the serious drug world. It was the beginning of the ride downwards right to the gates of hell where he sold his soul to an unknown devil.

In a few weeks, our dear friends Mark and Marty would be joining us for the weekend. All of us including Dane would be going to attend the "Regeneration Tour". Slated for August 24, 2008 the tour was made up with some of our favorite '80's bands, scheduled to perform. Dane had read about the show and insisted that we all go together. We gave him permission to order the tickets online. How cool was it that Flock of Seagulls, Belinda Carlisle, Naked Eye, Human League and ABC would all share the stage? Mark is an old friend of mine from Alpena and Marty was his partner in life and in crime. The two of them made a wonderful couple although to look at them they seemed polar opposites. Mark is a tall guy with a wonderful sense of fashion-always decked out impeccably while Marty was an old punk rocker with a Goth vibe. They loved each other and got on like Laurel and Hardy and generally made everyone around them giggle in delight. Everyone loves having them around and Dane was no exception.

Ever since he was a little boy, Mark treated him to candy and other goodies in an amount that I never approved of. They were totally conspiratorial as party bags of M&M's and ice cream were consumed. Marty and Dane had the same taste in cheeseball movies and would sit in our living room and watch them one after the other. They also shared a love of music and would debate the merits of all genres. They bonded in their love of early punk music and their shared hatred of country music. Dane called them his uncles and insisted that Mark and Marty were his godfather's. He was highly protective of them. He loved them and was looking forward to enjoying the concert with them.

But something didn't seem right. Dane was alternately manic and then irritable. He was sweating bullets on this temperate night. I caught him dozing off at one time during the show and elbowed him hard. "What's the matter with you? Did you take your meds? Didn't you sleep last night?" He answered that he did, just not very well. I decided to ignore him and watch the show. After the concert, we all piled into Randy's truck and drove home. We were all jabbering on about the great show, except for Marty who was uncharacteristically quiet. It was nearly midnight when we all went to bed. Marty went upstairs without his usual nightcap.

On Monday afternoon, Randy called me to suggest that we go out for dinner. Never one to turn that down, I put the roast I was preparing into the refrigerator for the next night. As I got myself ready to go out Dane was napping in his room when we left. We drove the short distance to the Engine House and were seated in front near the window. Situated near the train tracks, the bar gave away free jello shots every time the train went by. We were sipping our wine when we heard the familiar whoo whooo, and the perky waitress dropped off our two shots. We tongued out the sweet treat and started to look over the menu. It was at that time that Randy said, "I've got something that I have to tell you and it's very serious. Marty called me this afternoon. He hated to betray Dane's trust but he felt we had to know. Dane is using heroin."

This time, the bottom truly did drop out of my world. I remember feeling nauseated and the room seemed to spin. "There must be some mistake. I would know if he was using heroin, wouldn't I? Why does Marty think that?" Randy sighed and said that Marty saw him snort it in the basement and at the concert. Marty was torn between his loyalty to Dane and his concern for him. He hoped that Dane would someday be able to forgive him and realize that this betrayal was for his own good.

I will never forget my despair at those words. Needless to say, I didn't bother to order dinner that night. Pot I could reluctantly accept, but how in the hell did he ever make the jump to heroin? I just could not fathom the gravity of this news. Did Dane not realize the addictive nature of that damn dangerous drug? With his OCD as well as his other mental health issues, this was very serious.

What on earth is the next step to stop this new madness? My head was spinning and I couldn't think straight. I was scared to death. I tried to recall everything I had ever heard or read about the drug, and none of it was good. I remembered that Dane had an appointment with his therapist the next day. Maybe I should call her and see what she would advise. Randy thought this was a good idea, so I stepped outside and made the call. As I dialed her phone number, I prayed that she would pick up her phone after hours. I was relieved when she answered and listened, as I told her of the situation. She advised that we have a family session tomorrow at 9:00 a.m. She also said that we should not say anything to Dane regarding this plan. It would be better if he did not have a chance to get on the defense. I agreed and said that we would see her in the morning. Confident that we had professional help on our side, I felt a modicum of relief. Drug lesson number one had officially began.

Upon arriving home, we found Dane watching television upstairs in the living room. Although he had a television in his basement bedroom, he often joined us upstairs to catch a movie or sporting event. The plate he was finishing indicated that he had microwaved some leftovers for his dinner. "Hiya Mom and Pops. How was dinner? The Tigers are leading, come watch the end with me." It was all we could do to remain cool and not approach that awful subject that was on the tip of our tongue. I searched his face for some sign that he had changed somehow. Not one thing seemed amiss in his appearance or demeanor. The rest of the evening was uneventful as we watched the Tiger's pull off the win. Before long, we all headed off to bed. Better try to get some rest, tomorrow was going to come soon enough.

The next morning, I met Dane at the coffee pot. "We are going with you to see your doctor this morning." I explained that his psychologist thought it was time we have a family meeting to evaluate his progress. Dane shrugged, "okay, sounds good." By eight thirty, we were all dressed and set to go. Randy and Dane rode together in Randy's truck and I followed in my car. Randy could go into work from Southfield and Dane and I would come home. The traffic was heavy in rush hour and we made it to the appointment in just the nick of time.

The doctor had Dane stay in the waiting room and called Randy and I into her office. She invited us to have a seat. She asked us how we knew what we heard was true. I explained to her that our source was a family friend. Any information from him was absolutely unquestionable. We were confident that what Marty said was the truth. A few more questions and it was time for Randy and I and Dane to switch places. With no clue as to what he was about to encounter, Dane joined her in her office. We were surprised when a few short minutes later, the doctor called us back in. "Dane says that it's not true," she informed us. "Don't lie, Dane. Uncle Marty called Randy and he was very concerned." Knowing that it would be useless to pursue this avenue any further, Dane finally came clean. " Fine, I've been using since the fourth of July weekend. "

Okay, so now we would need details. Dane explained that the weekend when he left the beach house early, he went downtown, (Detroit) and bought the drug. He told us that he was only snorting the drug-a practice much less dangerous than using a needle. It was also much less addictive that way and besides, his lifelong fear of needles kept him away from injecting the drug. I asked him what made him buy heroin on that day. He replied that he just needed something extra and that the pot doesn't always work. "It's no big deal," Dane assured us. However; we were far from assured. I angrily informed him that if he didn't stop immediately he was going straight into a rehab-do not pass go! Naively, at this time, I thought he could 'just quit'. "Fine, mom, I'll stop. You don't have to freak out about it." I ranted on a little more, thinking that I could actually make a difference in his thinking. "You know the rules, no drugs EVER in our house. Not allowed. I will be watching you like a hawk."

We left the office and drove home in complete silence. I was sick to my stomach from all of this. Dane broke the ice by asking if we could take a run through McDonald's for a cheeseburger. Historically, in good times and bad, a cheeseburger and chocolate shake were his go to comfort food. I pulled over at the nearest golden arches and we went through the drive in and picked up his brunch. I finally broke my silence and said, "Dane, are you even kidding me? Heroin is a drug I never would have thought you would try. People die from it. I'm sure just purchasing it must be dangerous. I thought you were smarter than that. I want to know everything. I cannot understand how you would take such a risk. Don't you have enough health issues? This needs to go away right now." Of course the "I know, Mom" was the inevitable answer.

Once again, I took to the internet to give myself a little education on the creature that I never thought I would have to become so intimately aware of. I studied the medical sites, and even read some personal blogs written by addicts. You Tube showed me how to snort it or cook the drug and inject it. Various people were interviewed and they all had one thing in common. Not one of them ever expected to become addicted. Sometimes rehabs don't work or takes more than one try. Many never fully recover. Once you are an addict, you are always an addict. There was not one single thing I read or saw that was the least bit reassuring. Now I was more scared than ever.

The next few months had Dane on his best behavior. He was engaged in family events and even helped me with some yard work-and he hates yard work. He looked good and fit and walked Mickey most days. I asked him every day if he was okay. I wondered if he really was not using. It just seemed too good to be true. But something still was niggling at me. I never saw the signs before and what if I didn't see them now? "I'm cool, Mom. Everything is okay. I love you, but you worry too much." A big hug and a kiss and he and Mickey were out the door for a little walk. Dear God, I prayed, let this be just a bump in the road. Please let us come away from this unscathed and healthy. Let this just be a hard lesson, well learned.

A few days later, Randy and I were getting ready to go to the Keys for a quick vacation. Dane would stay home with Mickey and see his doctor that managed his psych medicines as well as attend his therapy appointments. He would work part time where Jeannie could keep an eye on him and then go up to my mom and dad's for a long weekend. I have always trusted that he would take good care of the house for us. He faithfully did his dishes and laundry and has always been a little nutty about the cleanliness of his bathroom. He folded his clothes to look like a shelf at the Gap, very much the perfectionist. So as we headed off that day, I thought that things were finally smoothing out. Daily calls-and usually more than one, kept us in constant contact. Dane sounded positive and I was almost sure that we had put this episode behind us. Once again, I had it all wrong.

Dane seemed to muddle through the first part of the week with no incident. On the weekend he packed up Mickey and his cat and headed up to Ossineke. It would be healthy for him to be in a different environment. Some fresh air along with the love from his Grammamom and Grampa would surely do the trick. Mom would welcome him and tolerate his pets for an extended stay. By now he had rescued a small flea bitten kitten from our shrubs. The kitty was orange and white after a bath, and Dane patiently loved him into submission. He named him Jaco, after the musician Jaco Pastorius famous for his long lines and incredible electric bass solos. Mom would walk Mickey-or rather Mickey would walk Mom. She would be counted on to cook all of Dane's favorite foods and desserts. He would eat many, many of her chocolate chip cookies. Dad would welcome the visit and look forward to their political discussions. The young Democrat and the old Republican could really heat things up as they solved the world's problems and lovingly agree to disagree. They would also watch old western movies ad nauseum on television. All three of them would cheer on their beloved Detroit Tiger's. Aunt Lisa could be counted on to welcome him at her restaurant and treat him to whatever he wanted on the menu. She would serve him the largest pieces of dessert in the house. He was comfortable visiting Rosa's and flirting with Tracey, his favorite waitress. He would visit my brother, Steve and his sons who lived nearby. I would be relaxed knowing he was in the loving arms of family.

Nearing the end of our vacation, I got the call that stopped me cold and dimmed the sunshine for me on that gorgeous Keys day. Mom called and I could tell by her voice that something was really bothering her.

Reluctantly she had to tell me that she walked in on Dane using a needle to inject heroin. Later, she was able to search his duffle bag and found more needles and paraphernalia. She hated to ruin our vacation, but felt we needed to know so we could plan in advance how to handle this. I could not believe it. Dane had always been scared to death of needles. I had to actually hold his hand during routine injections.

He would turn snow white and threaten to faint every time! But Mom said she was absolutely positive of what she had seen. Needless to say, my false sense of precariously fragile security had once again been shattered. I was sick with worry and had to tell Randy as soon as he got in from fishing so we could somehow come up with a plan.

After relating the story to Randy, we decided that when we got back home, we would go up to Ossineke and do a full on surprise intervention on Dane. I would read everything I could get my hands on as well as get advice from his therapist on exactly how to accomplish this. We would give him no other choice than to go to a rehab. He would not be allowed to live at our house or work at the company if he was using heroin. None of my family would support him in any way other than recovery. My whole family was apprised of the situation and were there to support us. He simply would have nowhere to run. Walking into my parents' home, I met a very surprised Dane. "What are you doing here? I didn't expect to see you. How was your vacation?" Of course, we shared a big hug and a kiss. We had earlier decided to meet up out at my sister and brother-in-law's house in Hubbard Lake. Trying to appear that everything was normal was not easy, but we had done it before.

Soon Mom, Lisa and Steve, my brother Steve, along with Randy and I were seated around the table that gave a beautiful view of the woods. The tension in the air was thick as all of us were a little nervous. My Dad was pacing around, a reluctant party to anything he perceived as negative towards his precious 'grand buddy'. Presently, Dane walked in and we asked him to take a seat. I started out with telling him that we all knew he was using heroin and that he had progressed to using a needle. I told him that rehab was the only choice that was left to him. He would not be allowed to live at our home or my parent's home. We were all hopeful for his future if he would just commit to treatment. It was that simple. Dane was clearly uncomfortable, and totally blindsided. His face flushed with embarrassment. But he didn't even try to deny anything. Realizing we were completely united and serious, sullenly, he agreed to treatment.

It was a very quiet dinner at Moms that night with everyone emotionally spent. We made small talk with the details of our vacation. Later Randy and I decided to take Mickey for a walk. We convinced a very quiet Dane to join us. Ossineke beach is one of Dane's very favorite places and we spent most summers there walking the sugar sand beach and swimming in the chilly waters of Lake Huron. It is absolutely beautiful there, with gentle waves rolling in. Walking along, I could tell that Dane was feeling remorseful. "I'm so sorry Mom and I'm sorry and embarrassed that Gramma had to see that. I have really fucked things up and I will do whatever it takes to get off this drug and get healthy again. I love you all and never meant to hurt you."

"Good" I sighed. "It won't be an easy journey, but we'll support you and get you the help you need."

I thanked God and the stars that we caught this as soon as we did. Early detection addiction, like most diseases increases the chances for recovery. We would blast this thing full on whatever it would take! But, I needed to figure how just how to do this. Lesson number two was now underway. The next morning after breakfast we all headed back home. I got on the computer immediately and searched drug rehabs.

Learning how rehabs work and navigating the red tape involved was arduous and confusing. I made some calls and didn't much like the answers I got. Dane was not prioritized because he had been using such a short time. "...But isn't that the whole point?" I countered. "I want this treated before it gets any worse." Unbelievably, I could find no open beds anywhere in Michigan. I got on a couple of waiting lists and would be notified if there were any changes. I called those toll free numbers that you see on television and learned that their programs start at $20,000.00. Tomorrow I would call our family doctor and apprise him of the situation. Hopefully he would have a recommendation. At dinner that night, I told Randy of everything I encountered in my fruitless search. Sweet and sympathetic as usual, he said that he would do everything in his power to help fix Dane. He was very disappointed in Dane and incredulous that help was so unavailable.

Living in the same house as Dane would prove to be a challenge as I looked at him with leery and scared eyes. But I didn't really have any choice. I was a nervous wreck but there was nothing much to do but helplessly wait. It turned out that Dane took care of the situation in his own way.

I took Mickey out to get the morning paper and settled in with my coffee and daily crossword and waited for Dane to come upstairs. When he didn't appear by noon, I went downstairs to check on him. His depression sometimes caused periods where he could barely get out of bed. I needed him to get up and help me with this rehab situation. It was equally his responsibility to help to find a treatment center. By the time he got up and had his coffee, half the day would be gone. With Mickey at my heels, we got to his bedside. I immediately knew something was very wrong. His breath was so slow and his face was very pale. His fingertips and lips were blue. He was actually cold to the touch; I rushed to call 911 and told them that my son was barely breathing and I think that he had overdosed. Not knowing what else to do, I began pounding on his chest in the area of his heart.

"C'mon," I begged," breathe again, please, breathe again." On his large coffee table near his candles, I saw various prescription bottles with their tops off and totally emptied out.

Within minutes, the Harrison Twp. Fire Department's emergency team was in the house, down the stairs and at Dane's bedside. "Do you know what he took?" "Yes, these prescriptions are all empty. I don't know how many pills there were in the bottles originally." They had put on oxygen and were taking Dane's vitals. When they asked me if I had a preference for a hospital, I told them to take Dane to St. John's Hospital. The ambulance showed up. Dane was loaded on a gurney and transported out of the door.

And then I saw it. A note was on his bedside table. I snatched it up and read. Dane explained that he loved us very much and could not stand to go on being a burden to us. He was sick of himself and tired of trying to live normally. He was sorry about his drug use. He wanted us to be happy. I simply could not comprehend Dane's actions. Putting the note in my purse, I would talk with him about it at the hospital. I got in my car and called Randy on the way. He left work and met me at the E.R. at St. John's.

When I got there a very morose Dane laid in a hospital bed. But he was awake and breathing. They had pumped his stomach. We exchanged a gentle hug. With tears rolling down, he said, "I'm so sorry Mom and Poppy. I am just sick and tired of everything. Your lives would be so much easier without the burden of me. You just don't deserve it." Of course, I told him not to be ridiculous. I loved him very much and could not image my life without him. Poppy could barely speak. Maybe an extended hospital stay with some more therapy could help. A social worker came in and asked for our insurance information.

She told us she would check our coverage and be right back. This whole thing seemed so surreal to me. My son had just tried to commit suicide. It was difficult to even process the thought. The social worker came back and told us that the mental ward stay would be covered at 50%. I fumed at the thought as I wondered if a cancer patient or heart patient would be covered at 50%. It was my first real experience with the frustration defining the reality of mental health treatment.

With that, Dane was moved to the mental health ward for an extended stay. Dane was completely compliant in this first hospitalization; a trait that would become normal for him. As he was rolled off to "E-1" we were informed of the rules.

Visiting days were Tuesday, Thursday and Saturday. He would be allowed to call us tomorrow. Randy and I hugged him one more time and Randy told him to stay strong. We would see him on the next visiting day. "I love you both very much" was his reply.

The next day Dane called and asked if I could bring him a few things to make his stay more comfortable. Could I please bring jeans, t-shirts, boxers and socks? He could wear tennis shoes as long as we took out the laces. Also he would like some of his books. He told me things were going fine. He had a shower and was feeling better. The nurses were nice. A pattern had begun. Dane would feel so secure in hospital stays that he sometimes appeared to not have a problem at all!

Routinely it appeared as if the doctors and staff would not take his condition seriously. Dane felt safe and somewhat happy when he was in a controlled environment. The medical profession was still very interesting to him, and he asked questions that always surprised the doctors. "Does he have a medical background?" they would ask as Dane read his monitors and questioned his medications. I told him that he had hopes of a career in the medical field. I made notes of his requests and packed a little bag to take to him. I told him that I would see him tomorrow and we exchanged our usual, "I love you".

I spent the rest of the morning on the phone with my family. Randy called his mom and brother with the details. Everyone was so concerned and supportive. I called Tony and told him what happened. Everybody wanted me to tell Dane to get well soon and that they would be thinking of him and praying for him. My Mom and Randy's Mom must have done a thousand laps on their rosary beads fervently praying for the recovery of Dane's soul.

The next day, I grabbed the duffel I had packed and made my way down I-94 to St. John's to visit Dane. I noticed a homeless man on the corner and noted to myself to bring him some food on my next visit. Lord knows what? The poor guy was probably addicted and/or mentally ill and probably had not eaten for a while. Later I was admonished by people for talking to the homeless people I encountered. They though these people were dangerous and would rob me or worse. But I never once felt threatened at any time. I had so much compassion for them and in the back of my mind I thought, "there but for the grace of God, go I." Never once, when giving a person food or money, did I feel in any danger. Giving them food or a few dollars was the very least I could do.

Arriving at the hospital, I learned that all visitors were required to have their bags searched and purses and keys had to be left at the desk after we signed in. We were not allowed in until exactly one o'clock when a guard let us walk, single file into the reception area. I was the first parent in the visitor line and thru the small rectangular window, I could see Dane pacing back and forth. The patients were instructed to take a seat in the cafeteria/social area. We visitors were marched in and I scanned the area until I spotted my son. When I finally got to Dane's table, I collected my bear hug and asked him how he was doing. "Good Mom, I'm doing good. Everyone here is very nice and tomorrow I will meet the therapist." We sat down and I wanted to have a conversation about what had happened.

I pulled the note out of my purse and laid it on the table between us. I had lots of questions. But Dane stopped me. "Mom, it was a mistake. I was very sad and I panicked. I will never do that again. Please don't worry. I am so sorry I worried you."

Dane ended up staying two weeks at the hospital and seemed to be getting stronger. His mood was good and he was participating in all group therapies as well as his individual ones. Three times a week, I brought him lunch from his favorite restaurants, not forgetting his cheeseburger and chocolate shakes. I was once again, very proud of him. The hospital had some news for us. They were recommending Brighton Hospital as an option for Dane's drug rehab. His bloodwork had shown dangerous levels of opiates and he qualified for treatment there. Brighton? Oh my God, I called there originally but they had no openings.

Brighton is a very renowned rehab facility known for it's positive results as well as it's prohibitive costs. Our social worker told us that our insurance would completely covered Dane's treatment there.

This stroke of financial luck turned out to be the first and only time we experienced full coverage on Dane's care.

The next morning, I remembered to grab a breakfast sandwich for the guy at the corner of I-94 and Moross. He probably would have rather had money, but it was apparent that he hadn't had exactly a healthy diet for a while. When I got to his spot, I put my window down and handed him the bag of food. "Have a nice day" I said and he replied with, "God bless you"

Minutes later I was at the hospital to pick up Dane. He was waiting as usual, and we went through the process of releasing him from the hospital. A brief meeting with Dane's doctor assured me that he had made a lot of progress and was completely stabilized. It was advised that if we had guns in the house we should consider moving them somewhere else or putting them in a safe; duly noted.

We have always had guns in the house, but now we could not take any chances. I was advised of the new meds they would be trying, to treat Dane's worsening depression. The staff was supportive and gathered around to wish him well. One of the male nurses hugged him hard and said, "Dane, you can do this. You are strong and smart. Go to Brighton and kick some ass. Make me proud, buddy." Dane smiled and told him, "I plan to and I hope to never see you again, dude!" As Dane and I walked across the parking lot to the structure he took a deep breath and announced that he was happy be outside breathing the fresh air. Moments later we located my car and I found myself back in the McDonald's drive thru collecting him his cheeseburger and chocolate shake.

Although Brighton Hospital was expecting us, I got permission to drive back home so Dane could visit his pets and pack a bag of necessities for his stay. Quickly we accomplished these tasks and were soon on our way west to the rehab. Dane was feeling almost as optimistic as I was. We called Poppy and gave him the update of the day. Pops wished Dane well and promised him that he would be at Brighton the very next visiting day. I asked Dane if he was nervous but he said he was almost relieved. He had heard of the reputation that the rehab had and promised to work hard on his issues. When we pulled into the parking lot both of us were pleasantly surprised at the beauty of the grounds. Brighton looks like a country club with its large groomed yard and paved parking lots.

Dane would be sent to a special area where they would make sure he was totally detoxed. I assured them that after his hospital stay there were no illicit drugs in his system and maybe this step could be skipped. It's procedure, I learned. After a few days he would be assigned a regular room and put on a schedule for classes, therapy, free time, meals and such. I was not able to tour the facility until visitor's day, but I was feeling assured that this was the right fit.

The professionalism at Brighton Hospital would be the best we ever encountered in the rehab realm. I was advised of the visiting schedule. Another hug from Dane, and I would leave him in their care. I must admit to driving away with a peaceful feeling that for a few more days, the house would be quiet and peaceful and Dane would be well cared for. It was such a stress relief for me to not be on constant patrol. There is much tension to be had living with a drug addict. We had started locking up anything that we felt had any value in a gun safe that Randy purchased, but I was still nervous. I feared that maybe he had friends that could threaten our safety. Dane later assured me that nobody knew where we lived. Well, I thought that provides some measure of relief.

Visiting days came and went and I was getting used to the drive to Brighton. As was his usual, Dane was always waiting to greet me, with a big smile and a giant bear hug. "You look good!" I couldn't believe how well he looked. Happily, I noted that his color looked normal and his eyes were clear and shiny. This must be a good sign. The rehab schedule for visitors was set up in the way that visitors and residents would split up and go to whatever class they were teaching on that day. We then would meet back up for a joint class followed by free time to visit and grab a snack.

I followed the group to my class and listened attentively while the instructor explained some of the processes the patients would be using to aid in their recovery. The class was very informative. It flew by and I realized then, that I had a lot of learning to do. This thing was so much bigger that anything we have ever done. I mentally noted that I was going to all of the classes Brighton offered as well as plenty of home study, determined to be an expert on Dane's addiction. Together we recited the short prayer that we were to hear in every rehab we ever attended. I prayed Dane would let this be his mantra. Without acceptance and acknowledgement of addiction we wouldn't stand chance. Class was dismissed and I set out to find my son.

Dane was always up for a snack and the snack bar already knew him well. "Hi, Dane. Large coffee and some M&M's?" the cute counter girl asked. "Mom, this is my girl. Get to know her cuz we probably will be married and have your grandbabies! She reads me like a book. This is my Mom and she wants a coffee, too." was Dane's reply. Smiling wildly and shaking her head she handed over our coffees with a "here ya go, hubby!" I paid the tab and we found a small high-top table in the common area to catch up. We sat down and sipped our coffee.

"Okay, Hon, tell me everything," I said. "This place is cool. The staff are amazing. The group meetings are structured—not just everybody talking bullshit. This one counselor, Mike is awesome. We've had some great talks. He works in the gym and I have been working out a little with him. I can't believe how good it feels to lift weights again!" I asked the normal questions regarding the food and how he was sleeping. I wondered if he had any one-on-one therapy yet. Dane assured that everything was fine and his new therapist was a woman that he felt comfortable talking to. He had only met with her once so far, but had another appointment scheduled. Now it was his turn to question me.

"What do you think of this place? Did you like the classes today?" he wanted to know. I started by speaking about the class we had taken together. The instructor asked all the parents if we had been lied to and stolen from our addicts. Most of us answered that we had. When the addicts were asked if they had ever lied or stolen from us, every one of them raised their hands.

The first stages of addiction are very similar in the fact that it is that start of the effect that includes the whole family. It was established that most of us parents are enabler's. I hate this word and did not believe it applied to Randy and me. Do we give him money? Sometimes. Do we let him drive our cars? Sometimes. Do we believe every excuse he gives us? Sometimes, again. But I argued, that we love him and want to help.

It seemed that all of us had the exact same lessons to learn. It can be argued that I did not support the addict but I did support my mentally ill son. The trick would be how to separate a problem so very intertwined. They were both parts that made up the person Dane was. I decided then that I would keep a tighter eye on the money and car mileage. My new job, for the time being would be a reluctant warden, detective, and parole officer, as well as mom, friend and caregiver.

I was absolutely shocked at how many young people were there getting treatment. At our group table, it was amazing how smart and attractive these kids were.

Meeting them anywhere else, you would never guess that their situation was one that was so dire. One of the boys expressed that he was leaving tomorrow and the first thing he was going to do, was get high. This shocked me. Another girl, the daughter of a local celebrity lawyer, was there on her third visit. She told me that her parents never visit, just dump her off and pick her up at the end of her stay. She even walked off once. The rest of them seemed to be working hard at their sobriety. Dane participated avidly in the class answering questions voluntarily.

Later I learned that there is a standard age measure found in most rehabs. The young people are most often heroin addicts. The middle aged women are usually addicted to prescription pills. Most of the older men and women are alcoholics.

A very hard fact that I learned was that heroin addicts have the shortest life span of all of the addicts. The life expectancy of a heroin addict is 31 years on average. By then an overdose, infection from dirty a needle, or organ failure takes their lives. They also put themselves at risk by buying their dope in dangerous areas. They sometimes drive when they are high. This is horrible I thought, numbly. But still naive in the reality of addiction; I never expected this grim fact would be so prophetic.

One visiting day, my Mom came along to see Dane. She brought him some of her chocolate chip cookies that he loved so much. Upon seeing her, Dane lit up like a candle and swooped her up in one of his hugs. They were so happy to see each other. Mom wanted to see for herself that he was getting help and she was eager to take the classes with me and try to understand how she could help. Off we went to our class with the promise to Dane to hook up to share coffee and cookies later. "Who says I'm gonna share?" he grinned as he walked down the hall. She felt that overall the experience was a real eye opener.

The class presentation demonstrated the seriousness of cravings and the odds for relapse. She shared my amazement at the young, normal looking kids who were addicts there for help. She and I would sit up with Randy later, discussing everything we learned.

And then I got some good news. The social worker called me into her office for a quick meeting. She informed me that they got an extension for Dane. He would be allowed 2 additional weeks of treatment, and insurance agreed to pay. The staff strongly recommended that we should take advantage of this. Well, of course, we would! I wouldn't even give Dane an option.

Turned out I wouldn't have to-Dane was as excited as I was about the extra stay. It was a tremendous relief and I hoped that the extra time would provide the education and support Dane would need. I had already been experiencing a niggling feeling that 9 days was not enough time to 'fix' Dane. He was learning tools, skills and behavior modification he would need to 'just say no'. And since I was still taking every class they offered, my lessons were able to continue as well. The group meetings were intense at every session. I simply had no idea how very deep the addiction struggle dives. If only it were ever as easy as "just say no."

Dane had seemingly made amazing progress and had made friends with all of the techs, counselors and therapists. They hugged and bumped fists every time they passed each other. "Hey, Buddy. How ya doin?" was the normal exchange. Once when Dane and I were seated during free time, a tall, handsome man in a nice suit stopped by, Dane and he embraced. He sat down for a moment and introduced himself. He told me that my son was doing wonderfully. He allowed that Dane was a very active participant and a natural leader. Smiling like an idiot, I proudly thanked him. After telling Dane how very proud I was of him, I asked him about that articulate man. "Oh yeah, Mom, he's a former addict. Got cleaned up in here and got into counseling. Most of the people here are formers." Wow, I never would have guessed. What a ray of hope that man provided me that day.

Most people that unfamiliar with addiction, especially heroin, tend to easily label the person. The poor wretches that we see on the side of the expressway, begging on the street, or living under the bridges and overpasses are too easy to judge. Instead, in treatment you will meet an entirely different looking addict.

Normal intelligent kids from every walk of life; some came from families as loving as ours, others were fighting this on their own and for them especially, I always felt sorry. I didn't see how they could possibly make it without strong family support. Some of them were there court mandated, and those were the ones that had a chip on their shoulder with no intention of staying clean. They were sometimes vocal in their intentions and I warned Dane to stay clear of them. Dane expressed that they sometimes wasted everyone's time in classes with their bad attitudes. I made friends with some of these kids and was able to question them.

A few had just meant to experiment with heroin once at a party and got hooked. A couple of them had a surgery and were prescribed OxyContin that lead to buying heroin. Others had stolen meds from friends and family medicine cabinets and got addicted to opioids. For the most part, they were all very remorseful and would have done anything to change the hurt they inflicted on their families as well as themselves. It was very troubling for me to hear these stories. Some of them were there on their second or third stay and were determined to beat their demons this time.

In one of my classes, they showed a movie called **Pleasure Unwoven by** . **Kevin McCauley** This was an award winning piece that explained how addiction had finally been qualified as a disease. The common feeling is that addiction is a choice and one must simply choose not to use-as if it could ever be that easy! The movie breaks down the problem in that theory. The first time a person uses, is the last time it is their choice. Addiction is a brain disease. Drugs and alcohol simply change the brain. The way addiction starts are this: very quickly the drug changes the paths to the pleasure center. A new route is carved out, one that supersedes even the most basic of brain functions. Food, water, sex and survival will now come in second to the need of the drug-addiction is that such a powerful force.

After stopping using the drug, it can take three months for the brain to heal these channels. It is very difficult, but it is possible. This movie was amazing and I recommend it to any parent of an addict. It will help you to understand addiction as well as educate others. We must work hard to dispel the "choice" argument if we are ever to get more drug awareness. No disease is ever a choice and addiction is a disease.

Three and a half weeks after his first rehab began it was time for my last drive to Brighton. Dane's rehab was complete and after today's classes, he would be released. Randy and I attended the last big group meeting that was being led by Dane's favorite leader and gym buddy-Mike.

Mike had us all seated in a large circle. He stood in the middle and spoke of how we needed to get in touch with the feelings that living with an addict made us experience. As he pointed at us for answers, he asked, "but, how does it make you feel?" Answers varied with "sad", "helpless", "angry" and other words of frustration. When Mike pointed to me I had tears in my eyes and a lump in my throat. "How do you feel?" he queried me. "Shattered", I managed to croak out.

My heart and dreams for my son's life were shattered by his addiction. Mike nodded his head and said, "Shattered is exactly what you feel. Like a mirror, your life is broken into pieces, much like a shattered mirror.

As parents of addicts it is our job to try to pick up the pieces of our lives, get strong and healthy and become whole again. Addiction is a family disease and you, my friends, are the collateral damage." Those words were exactly my truth and still resonate with me even today.

It was recommended that constant outpatient therapy as well as Narcotics Anonymous meetings attended. He had in his possession phone numbers he could call in case of emergency. Dane said his goodbyes and many hugs and back pats went around that circle. It was re-affirmed that he was strong, smart, and ready to move on with his life-clean. I was very proud and happy for him. Surely this was the start of new things and a better life.

As we collected Dane's duffel and walked across the parking lot I noticed that he was quiet and he had tears streaming down his face. Always an emotional kid, I just figured that he was sad to leave some of the people that had impacted him. "You okay?" I asked. Dane looked at me and said, "I'm scared Mom. I'm not ready. It wasn't long enough. I don't feel that strong." I felt sick to my stomach even thinking of the possibility. Poppy and I will help you. You can do this. When we get home let's figure out a meeting schedule for you. It's gonna be okay." Miserably, Dane answered with a slight nod of his head. Later Dane explained to me that part of his sadness was a side effect from coming off of the drug. He learned in Brighton about something called 'anhedonia'.

Anhedonia, he explained was the inability to experience pleasure in things that normally give you happiness. He was worried that he would be unable to ever find joy again in doing the things he loved. What if his pets, music, family and friends couldn't help him to sustain joy? He was so very sad. I choked out a reply. "Don't worry, honey. Together we will find your joy; if it's the last thing I ever do."

Dane just sighed.

Somewhere in this story I must insert the sad reality of theft. It is sometimes the very first sign that you will notice if your child is in drug trouble. The addict usually simply cannot afford his expensive new habit. At first they may drain their savings and checking accounts. Sometimes they sell electronics and collectibles.

As the habit increases so does the cost. It may take extra gas money to drive to get the fix. Work usually suffers and there is less income than ever. As parents, hopefully we are watching a little more closely. And it we aren't, we should be.

Randy and I had suspected that we were missing some money from our wallets, just a little here and there. I once put a note in Randy's wallet that read "thou shalt not steal and this means you, Dane." He was very sheepish after that one. A large jar of change in Randy's closet gradually was emptied of all of his quarters as well as the coin keeper in his truck. Still we were unaware of how bad the thieving could become. One time I had purchased a pair of Tag Heuer sunglasses for Randy's birthday. He had admired them once and I was excited to be able to gift them to him. Those glasses along with the first pair of really nice prescription glasses that I ever owned disappeared.

Dane would forever vehemently deny that theft. We believe he simply didn't remember doing it. Randy had a tub of hunting clothes come up missing as well as some tools. Gas cans full of gas, disappeared from our garage.

I think it was at this time when Dane was newly home from Brighton Hospital that Randy got us tickets to catch a pre-season Detroit Red Wings game. Never a huge hockey fan, I still enjoyed all the crazy pageantry as well as the traditional dinner in Greektown before the game. I dug out my Red Wing colors and got ready to go and blow off a little steam. A fun date night with Randy maybe would help me forget about the mess we were living in. Randy would be home from work early and we would head downtown for the festivities. We were ready to rock when a thought occurred to me.

Wait-I almost forgot! I needed my gold omega chain with the ruby and diamond slide that Randy bought me a few years ago as well as the matching earrings and ring. Rubies are my birthstone and their red color is perfectly "Red Wings" red. I went upstairs and opened up my jewelry box. Hmmmmm, I thought, why does this seem so empty?

Why, can't I see that large gold necklace? Sickly, I realized that it was all gone. My tanzanite ring and earrings, along with a tanzanite and diamond bracelet, the opal and diamond bracelet, were also missing. The custom-made spessartite ring I got at the Ann Arbor art fair. A simple gold interlocking heart bracelet that was the first piece of jewelry that Randy ever gave me was missing as well. Various other gold chains were gone. All that was left was the costume stuff.

Breath came hard as I went back down the stairs, nauseated with the fact that Dane assuredly had stolen it. I yelled down to his room, "Dane, get up here right now. I need to talk to you!" He appeared immediately with a "what's up, Mom?" I quietly explained that all my jewelry was gone. "What do you mean?" was his reply. Dane has never been a good liar and this time was no different although later he would become a pro. I could see in his pale face that he was guilty. "Just admit it, you took my jewelry." He looked me straight in the eye and confessed, "Yes, I took it." 'What in the hell were you thinking and how can I get it back?" I asked him angrily. He was very embarrassed as he answered, "You can't, Mom. I pawned it."

I grabbed his arms and saw the fresh track marks, I had all the answers I needed. "What do you have to say for yourself, Dane? Some of those things were very special to me and gifts from Poppy." By now we were both crying as he tells me, "Mom, you were in Florida and I was so sick. I just had to get right. I knew it was wrong even as I was doing it, but I thought that I would just pay you back someday." I had no words. There was no sense in ruining Randy's night too, and I decided to tell him later. I wasn't sure if he could ever forgive Dane. It would prove to be a challenge for me as well.

Over the next few years, we slowly realized that we were missing other things. He never touched our electronics-an easy pawn shop trade. Dane stole some jewelry from my Mom that she forgot to hide as well as money from her wallet. I found some fake gold chains in his room once and I can guess that they were stolen and attempted to pawn. What a day that must have been as he got the news that the goods were worthless.

Later, we found out from friend and jeweler extraordinaire, Kara, that sometimes the pawn shops and police work together in returning things. We never reported the theft, though. Gold was at an all-time high and the pieces would have immediately been melted. The semi-precious stones would have been incidental to the gold money. I suspect that somehow more crimes were being committed as time went on and his habit increased.

Dane once told me that he had done many bad things and was never caught. He seemed deeply ashamed, but driven by a much larger need. I'm sure he stole from others as well as sold his plasma-a common way to earn an easy $100.00. All this was so disheartening because Dane was formerly one of the highest principled people I had ever known.

Addiction changes all of that as the drug prioritizes itself over even strongly held morals. It's so very sad.

PAWN SHOP WOMAN

High steppin' to the pawn shop

Walkin' round

Lookin' down on everyone

in the town.

Just a pretty girl high steppin' into the pawnshop

Open up your purse

to see what's there

When there ain't nothin' left

You end up sellin' yourself

Quick cash and a third of what your worth

Another good lookin' woman

walkin' out the pawnshop.

©Dane Jacobs

The counselors at Brighton Hospital recommended that Dane use intensive outpatient therapy (IOP) to help him stay on track. Using his list of phone numbers and N.A. locations, Dane would have to commit to aftercare. A local hospital offered sessions that ran from nine to one o'clock every day. The program was to include private and group therapy sessions as well as A.A. and N.A. meetings. After attending for 5 days, Dane dropped out. The patients did arts and crafts and no therapy sessions were ever held.

Innocently, Randy and I thought that we were on the right track to Dane's rehab. He now had some skills and resources to fall back on and we thought his conviction to stay clean was renewed. His favorite Brighton counselor attended N.A. meetings in a church near our home and Dane was comfortable having Mike there. Dane would eat dinner and head out to a meeting. Sometimes they would go out for a bite afterwards and we were pleased to see Dane engaging with others on the same journey as he was. He seemed optimistic and was even able to go back to work part time. I was proud to see him dressed in jeans, an R.S. Dale tee shirt and his faithful Doc Martens, filling his travel mug and heading out.

But it wasn't long before we noticed things slipping out of control once again. One Sunday morning, Dane came upstairs in his boxers and we met up at the coffee pot. I noticed some red streaks on the inside of his arms near his elbow joint. I grabbed both of his arms, "what the hell are these streaks?" I demanded to know. "Oh they are nothing. I helped a friend move from an upstairs apartment and I got these carrying heavy things down stairs." I was suspicious and told him that those better be healed in a day or two. In hindsight, I cannot believe I fell for this transparent explanation; being new and not yet fully educated to the situation made me trust Dane. I wasn't used to him lying.   Yet.

A few mornings later, Randy let Mickey out the back door to do his morning thing. Taking his phone with him, Randy sat on the steps of the deck and made a call. During his conversation, he happened to notice something catching the light by the holly bush. What he saw next blew his mind. Cutting his conversation short, Randy reached down and picked up a syringe that was lying in plain sight. Collecting Mickey, he came back in the house and called for Dane to come upstairs immediately. I came down from my room and Randy incredulously filled me on this latest event. Sensing that his Poppy meant business, a sleepy Dane came trudging up the stairs and did the 'Frankenstein walk' to the coffee pot. Calmly, Randy waited for him to sit down at the bar before he asked for an explanation. But, this time there was none.

No lie could possibly cover the evidence. We both ranted and raved with all the useless and ineffective things you could possibly think of. Tears started flowing as he explained that although he was trying to stop, he was using again. Fuming, Randy said that Dane would have exactly 8 hours to figure out what he was going to do. He would not be allowed to live in our home using and carelessly leaving needles lay around. I was furious and informed him that he was not to leave the house under any circumstances today, and it was his job to search out another rehab. Dane asked for some time alone to think. He would come back up later to join me in a phone search. I reminded him again, rehab was the only option for him if he wanted Randy and I's support. He would under no circumstances be welcome here otherwise. Dane nodded resignedly. I skipped my gym workout that morning and stayed home. I was too shaken and defeated to do anything.

Now I had become a reluctant security guard, guarding my home and my troubled prisoner.

About an hour later, I could hear Dane moving about in his room. He came up and got a shower, and went back downstairs. I assumed he would be back up to get on the phone and start our search. I was surprised to see him with his jacket on and carrying a large duffel bag. "Where are you going?" I asked. He replied, "just gonna stay with some friends. I'll call you when I get settled." We heard a car honk in the driveway and when I looked out; I saw a Shamrock cab waiting. Dane came over to me and gave me a giant hug. "Don't worry Mom, I'll be fine. Please take care of my pets for me until I can figure some things out. I love you." With that, he was out the door, in the cab and on his way to parts unknown.

I was in utter shock. I could not imagine what friend would allow him to stay with them. Without his job, he would run out of money soon. Oddly, as nervous as I was, I felt that relief that comes with not being responsible for Dane. The pressure was starting to get to me; even though I feared for his safety.

I hoped that maybe he would learn some sort of lesson. Maybe he would "hit bottom" and decide to get clean for real. I called Randy at work and told him that the 'solution' actually came pretty fast. He expressed that he too, thought it might teach him a lesson or two. It was his choice and we would just have to wait and see how this would shake out. God knows where he was off too and the probable dangerous situation he was putting himself in. Worried sick, neither of us slept that night.

A few days passed and I still didn't hear from Dane. I was getting more nervous by the minute. I was petrified that something had happed to him. I half expected the hospital to call any moment-or worse. Randy and I decided that we would not call him. He knew our rules and hopefully by waiting for him to call us, a choice would be indicated. I jumped out of my skin every time the phone rang, fearing the worst case scenario that I played over and over in my head. Randy suggested that we get out of the house and go to Luigi's for dinner and try to relax. Sipping our wine, we tried to talk about anything but Dane and our worry. Just then, I heard my cell phone ringing in my purse. I quickly pulled it out and saw that the caller I.D. showed Dane's phone number. Hoping for the best and fearing the worst, I answered. Dane's voice cheerfully said, "Hi Mom! How are you?" He went on to say that he was doing fine and staying with some friends in Highland Park. Things were going well. He had been to the casino a couple of times and had won some money. He wanted to know how Poppy and his pets were and that he would be home to visit us all very soon.

Stunned, I hung up my phone. I couldn't believe that he sounded that good; but—Highland Park, the casino? What the hell? There was nothing good about Highland Park. It is a rough area that we always avoided. Well, Randy and I did, at least. And what was this nonsense about gambling? Dane had never shown any interest in the casino. He always loved getting scratch off lottery tickets but I had never known him to even purchase one. I learned much later that he could count cards. I was not surprised at this revelation. He was a genius and could remember anything he saw or read. The conversation was short and I didn't have the mental presence to ask him any more questions. Randy and I were relieved that he seemed safe. But we were not at all thrilled with this development. We again reassured ourselves that these were choices Dane was making. Maybe he needed to fall down again. This tough love thing was just that-tough, tougher on us or Dane is the question.

A few days later, I came home from the gym and noticed that the door to the basement was open. As I went down the stairs I noticed his duffel bag first. As I rounded the corner, there was Dane sleeping peacefully with Mickey and Jaco curled up beside him. I couldn't believe he just showed up without calling me and went down to sleep as if it was business as usual. I sat down on his bed and shook him awake. "Wake up, you've got some 'splainin' to do."

Slowly he woke up and sat up in bed. He gave me a hug and stated how good it was to be in his own bed. "Mom, it was just awful. I can't live like that. I will go to the first rehab we can find. I'm done. I have to get clean. I am so sorry for making you guys worry. You don't deserve it and I don't like who I am anymore. I'll get a shower and some coffee and then I'll get right on the phone. Sighing, I told him and that I would help him. I set off to make coffee and he got his things together for a shower.

Soon we had the computer at hand as well as pens and notepads. The search was on. We found a place called Harbor Oaks and they would have a bed available that night or the next morning at the latest. Dane needed to do some laundry in preparation and went downstairs to get his dirty clothes. After starting the washer, he came back to sit and talk. I wanted some details of his time away. Where did you stay? What did you eat? Who were these friends? How did you pay for things? He explained that there are houses in Detroit that you can rent a corner for ten dollars a night. You pay the money and they show you a spot to put your things. You can sleep on a filthy mattress or the dirty floor. The "residents" take turns watching each other's possessions from the theft that would surely occur otherwise. He said the house was large and there were about 20 people coming in and out.

All types of scamming and drug use were going on. Liquor bottles, needles and crack pipes littered the floors and the place smelled horrible. An un-showered bunch of people soiling themselves amongst the garbage, did not make for a pleasant odor. Horrified, I asked him if he was scared. "Not really." was his answer. As a man who always enjoyed order as well as the creature comforts of life, he just couldn't stand the filth and disarray of everyone's stuff lying about. It was constantly noisy with no privacy and he couldn't sleep with one eye open. People hollered and hallucinated all day and all night long. They got into fist fights and argument. He couldn't stay as hygienic as he was used to. And he was exhausted to the bone. I could barely believe what I was hearing. So he called a cab and returned home. Drugs could really drive you make living choices such as this? Unreal.

Dane finished his laundry that afternoon and we waited for the call from Harbor Oaks to admit him to the rehab. Poppy came home and we all had dinner. Incredulously, Poppy listened to the same details that Dane told me earlier. In disbelief, Pops asked Dane if he had learned anything. Dane replied that he wanted a different life and would do the work to make that happen.

The call came in and Dane said goodbye to his pets. He grabbed the waiting duffel bag and the three of us piled into the truck. As we made the short drive to New Baltimore I told Dane he would need to work hard and participate fully. This was an expensive rehab and our insurance would not cover it. Please, I pleaded with him. Take this seriously. As usual, he was compliant and optimistic. While waiting, we met a very pregnant young girl that was obviously using. I offered up a silent prayer for her and that poor child. We proceeded through the admittance process and hugged Dane goodbye. On visiting day, we would be back.

Randy and I drove home and shared the thought that maybe this time would be different after the things Dane had recently experienced. Two days later when Randy and I went back to visit, a patient approached us with the offer for us to buy some drugs. I reported the boy to a counselor and felt very defeated.

Dane-26 years old

Upon Dane's release from Harbor Oaks, the counselor recommended that he continue treatment at a halfway house. I agreed that was clearly necessary because it was too hard having him live at home. I wasn't altogether familiar with the concept of a halfway house. The rehab was not affiliated with any particular one, so once again we had to do our homework. We were still far from being out of the woods regarding this addiction and the thought of an in house system seemed appealing.

The internet turned up one we were interested in. The Abaris system was one of the local organizations we found that also included a co-operating half way house. We noted the phone number and called to set up an interview as soon as possible. I had plenty of questions to ask. The director of the program told us that in addition to living in the house, residents would be treated with group therapy, psychological therapy, N.A. and A.A. meetings, as well as in house private sessions. A social worker would be available to make sure they were getting all the government aid (which is very little) that was available to them. Dane would be expected to provide his own food and help out with basic chores. We learned that a bed would be open in two days and we could come that very afternoon to see the home and discuss the program and the costs. Addresses of these homes, we learned, are almost always kept private. There is nothing obvious to the bare eyes that this was the nature of the house. The law protects the patient's privacy and anonymity.

This place known as 'Josh House' was located a short 15 minutes from our home, and an even shorter commute to R.S. Dale. Optimistically, we all jumped into the truck and drove over to discuss the details of getting Dane into the program. As always, Dane was completely co-operative. He was excited to try again in this new environment.

The house turned out to be a very large home with current availability to house 8 men. Dane would have a shared bedroom upstairs. There was a large kitchen and we were shown the cupboard where Dane could store his food. A big island in the middle could easily sit 10, and had a large bowl of fruit in the center. We saw the spacious living room complete with a fireplace and plenty of seating for viewing the large flat screen television. A job chart as well as a meeting schedule was posted on the wall. A very large yard with a bonfire pit held plenty of parking spots although most of the residents did not have cars-including Dane.

He would be allowed to leave for extended periods of time and sometimes even overnighters back home with a sign out/permission slip sort of system. Mickey would be allowed for overnight visits also, with clearance ahead of time. There would be random urine checks. As we heard the details, we relaxed a little, just knowing that this was the answer for extending Dane's treatment. And having him so close to home was a comforting bonus. Dane was happy and ready to embrace the program. With new confidence, Randy and I wrote another check for Dane's first month at Josh House.

We left the place in high spirits and drove back home. That night we decided what Dane would need and made a list of things. He packed his clothes, books, and toiletry items as well as his laptop and cell phone. We went over his grocery list. Of course, Randy and I would be enlisted to care for Mickey and Jaco. Mickey would be a welcome guest at Josh House soon enough. I could pick Dane up for lunch dates and grocery shopping and would sometimes be responsible for getting him to the therapy appointments in Rochester. The program also offered family therapy and Randy and I would attend that as well as a parent group meeting. Between the house phone and Dane's cell, it would be easy to keep up the constant contact that we were used to. I felt very secure in this structured plan, and God forbid, if it didn't work out, we would find something else.

I moved Dane in the next day and helped him set up his room. We then hit up Kroger and stocked up on some supplies. Luckily, Kroger and Rite Aid were a short walk from the house. I met the woman who was in charge of the day to day running of the house. I instantly liked her. A former addict herself-she was a take no bullshit kind of gal. She was tough and smart, having had so much experience herself. As Dane was putting his things away, she and I engaged in a long conversation. She had many questions regarding Dane's addiction and our role in his recovery. I filled her in on all we had experienced and the hospitalizations and rehabs he had been treated at.

She asked me if I was going to Nar Anon meetings and I told her that I hadn't done that yet. She said, "Mom, you need to break out of your own addiction." Huh? "My addiction, to what?" I asked. She smiled and said, "You are addicted to Dane. Love is your drug."

Wow. I had never looked at it that way. I was just doing what I had always done for Dane, making his world the best that I could. It was a shocking statement that I later would accept as the truth. Love WAS my drug. She explained that Dane needs to be on his own and suffer his consequences without the safety net that Randy and I provided him.

We needed to lead our lives and let Dane choose and live his. My head was spinning and I told her I needed to process this concept. She assured me that we would talk soon. And once again, I was forced to drive off and let someone else be responsible for Dane's care. I have to admit that I was hopeful and having a 24-hour professional team working with him felt very positive. Our house was quiet that night at dinner and I filled Randy in on all the details of the day. Cross your fingers and say a prayer-this just might work.

But now we had more lessons to learn. Even with random 'urine drops' as well as room searches, sadly, drugs were still being used in the house. There is no one any more cunning and scheming than an addict. The men could easily figure out the schedules of the house monitor and plan their use accordingly. The supervision just wasn't enough. Unless a drug or alcohol user is watched 24/7, they will seize the opportunity to use. And having a houseful of addicts trying to recover is really not a good idea. When things are going well, they do tend to support each other. There can be strength in numbers. But when even one of them wavers, it sets off a chain reaction that spreads like a California wildfire throughout the house. What one of them doesn't think of, the other ones will. And with a semi open door policy, visitors can bring contraband in the house most anytime. It was like herding cats trying to get all of the residents on the same page, at the same time, with the same positive goals.

In a short time, I got to know the other guys. I enjoyed bringing them all donuts and other treats. As a rule, addicts have the biggest sweet tooth of anyone I know. They simply seem to crave sugar. I think they are so accustomed to their pleasure centers being stimulated that sugar is the substitution for drugs and or alcohol. Being called 'Mom' by them was fine with me. I never once witnessed any of the others having someone in to visit them. I would drop by often and Dane and I would sit at the island and do crossword puzzles and chat for hours while he got his sugar fix. I was delighted to see him so happy and engaged. He didn't even mind his chores, but bitched that they didn't keep the kitchen and bathrooms as clean as he liked. Many times he just cleaned it himself. The little sunporch was also known as the smoking area. Dane also complained that he always had to walk through the smoke and his clothes smelled gross. Just deal with it, I told him as he Febrezed off his pea coat.

The subject eventually turned to his treatment. It was going well and he as well as all the other guys had little crushes on the manager as well as the social worker. Just be respectful, I warned. I suspected that all of them were a little lonely. A young girl named Nicole was serving an apprenticeship at

Josh House. She was in school studying social work and was in charge of the helping the men get government SNAP benefits, Medicaid and other services. All of the guys enjoyed having her around. Nicole helped to lighten up the mood in that house of men.

I loved that she engaged Dane in pumpkin carving and Christmas tree decorating. He proudly had me taste some pumpkin seeds they had roasted. Sometimes they played board games and had ice cream and movie nights. She was very sweet and caring and I'll always be thankful for her kindness to Dane.

I started to get very familiar with the other guys. One kid caught my attention immediately. "Joey" was about 21 years old and I just couldn't figure him out. He appeared totally mentally incapacitated. I asked Dane what Joey's D.O.C. (drug of choice) was. "Spice, Mom. Joey smokes spice" was his answer. Spice? The stuff you can buy over the counter that they were trying to ban from gas stations and party stores? Yep. I was able to witness firsthand the horrible effects of this drug. One day, I was visiting during breakfast time. Joey came into the kitchen. He opened the cabinet and took out his Cocoa Puffs. He then moved to the lower cabinet to get a bowl. He opened the door and peered in at the bowls. He closed the door without getting one. Joey repeated this at least three more times, not seeming to see the bowls that were right in front of him. He finally just gave up and sat down staring at the cereal box. I asked him if he needed a bowl. He nodded and I got up and retrieved a bowl. I watched as he opened the silverware drawer and look at the utensils as if he had never seen them before. He repeated the same open and shutting of that drawer. I walked over and picked him out a spoon. We located his milk and finally, Joey was able to eat his breakfast. It was a very sad thing to witness.

On another visit, I helped him make a sandwich and watched as he sat taking it apart, confused as to what to do with it. The drug had fried the circuits in his brain. It was a permanent condition from something that he had legally purchased. How very wrong and sad that was. Later Joey, was transferred to a mental hospital where they were more equipped to handle his problems.

Another resident was an elderly gentleman that was a longtime alcoholic. He was undergoing treatment that was court ordered after his fifth drunk driving offense. He really did not want to be there. Dane told me he was suffering from a condition known as 'wet brain', meaning his brain was literally pickled. This condition is caused by excessive alcohol abuse. Confusion, dementia, and hallucinations are the mental side effects as well as the fact that he could barely walk even with the assistance of a walker.

Dane was very sympathetic to both he and Joey's problems and took both of them under his wing. He hated to see either of them struggle and helped them whenever he could. Mickey also loved to sit by the man's recliner and be petted for hours. I think he sensed the fact that the man was very ill. It wasn't long before he somehow just walked away from the home. We learned later that he was back in jail. Heartbreaking.

Another roommate was a man from a very wealthy family; he had his own car, and was able to hold down a job. He just was unable to function on his own without bingeing on his D.O.C. He would use any drug that was available, as well as being alcoholic. It was not unusual for his family to pick him to treat him to dinner at some of the area's finest restaurants. He was cross addicted but seemed determined to make it this time. He had lived at the Josh House for a couple of years and had a few relapses. He was shy and seemed kind and Dane liked him immediately. Sadly, letting the boys borrow his car opened up a whole world of trouble as they could easily run out and find their drugs.

As addicts they all had sneaking and lying down to an art form. They would say they were going to a meeting and then have three whole hours to do what they pleased. Later the house required that they get signatures from the meeting leader, which they easily figured out how to forge. Failure to pass the urine drops were grounds for immediate suspension. It was easy for them to figure out how to get Joey to save his urine because the drug, spice, did not show up on the test. Sometimes it worked and other times the cold urine was questioned. Even though random room searches were conducted, it was rare that any contraband was found. The house monitor explained that they would have to have a drug sniffing dog to completely do the job. Addicts will take the batteries out of electronics and store dope in those spots. Toilets and sinks would have to be dismantled. It was almost impossible to make a clean sweep. They were an ingenious lot, those residents of Josh House.

Dane confessed all this to me when I questioned him on these policies. He reiterated that getting and staying clean was a personal commitment. I told him that I hoped it was, in fact, his commitment. He sighed and said he was doing his best.

One day Dane and I hit a nearby Mexican restaurant for lunch. Aubela's was a favorite spot of ours offering huge plates of nachos. Sharing an order, we caught up on things. Many giggles later, we were done with lunch. A quick stop at Kroger for some groceries and I took him back to the house. A hug, kiss and "I love you, Mom" and I was on my way. Shortly after I got home, I got a call.

A very upset Dane in tears and near hysteria said, "It's all gone, Mom. All my stuff is gone." "Slow down and tell me how they got in your room" I asked. He told me that his room was locked, but his window had been broken and his room was ransacked. Missing were his television, laptop, iPod, stereo equipment, his Doc Martens, and some of his clothes. I told him to calm down and I would make some calls and call him right back.

He set out to find the other guys to see if anyone knew anything. I called Abaris only to get an afterhours voicemail. I left my message and waited 15 minutes for a call back. Forty minutes after Danes call I was in my car and drove back to pick up the frantic and incensed Dane. He was threatening to harm one or all of the guys. He was positive that they knew who invaded his privacy and took his things. Arriving at Josh, I went upstairs and surveyed the mess. I took pictures of everything. Dane grabbed overnight things and signed out.

We went home and the stress of the situation had him asleep on the couch with Mickey in minutes. The next morning, I was able to explain the situation to the head of Abaris. He suggested that we file a police report. I asked if the house homeowner's policy would cover this theft and did not get a straight answer. We made a list and filed the report. Abaris never followed thru, and we never got any compensation. It was our loss and Dane took it very personally. I couldn't help but wonder if the irony of having your things stolen was realized by him. I went over and helped him clean up the incredible mess. Someone was there repairing the broken window. Later we learned that the robber was in fact, another one of the residents.

The boy was kicked out of the house and a week later committed suicide.

Dane took this time to renew his commitment to stay clean. He disengaged himself from the other guys as much as possible. When he was lonely we would arrange more visits home or I would bring Mickey over to him. He had been going to his meetings and reports from his counselors were that he was doing well and getting stronger. He had some clean time under his belt and was proud of it. Soon another one of the guys got caught violating and was asked to leave the house. Dane and another resident were going to help him move to a Knight's Inn south of Josh House in a rather shabby area. As you can imagine, this was not a good idea.

Dane agreed to help with the move and headed off with the boys. The next day I got a call from Nicole, the social worker, asking me if Dane had come home for a visit. He had not come back to Josh house the previous night and nobody had heard from him. I called his cell and it went straight to voicemail.

With that old sick feeling in my stomach, I waited anxiously by the phone. Later, Nicole called me and said that one of the guys in the house broke the creed and told her what had happened. She drove to the seedy hotel to discover that Dane had overdosed in the room and an ambulance had just left with him. The boys thankfully called 911 and split the scene without waiting for help to arrive. Worried for their own high asses, they still left him to die alone. Nicole called me and then she went to the nearest hospital and found Dane.

He was now stabilized and she insisted that he call me. If he didn't she warned him, she would make the call herself. My cell phone rang and I heard Dane say, "Mom, I'm okay. I had a convulsion." "Really? A convulsion? Don't even bother to lie Dane, I know you used." So once again, I was off to a hospital. I found his room where I learned that he had to have special care in the ambulance because he was so very close to dying. Resigned, Dane told me the whole story. I remarked at the loyalty and intent of the friends he was helping. He was stabilized and released the next day-business as usual for that hospital.

Due to his relapse, Dane was not let back into Josh House until he completed another inpatient rehab. I wasn't sure I wanted him there anymore anyway. I picked him up, got him his cheeseburger and shake and took him back home. While I fumed, Dane and Mickey slept happily through the night.

Trust me; I was not thrilled at this new turn of events. I really thought we were farther along than this. I was totally exasperated and did not know where to turn to next.

Dane's addiction was completely taking over our lives. The next morning found all three of us having coffee at our kitchen bar. It was decided that Dane and I would spend the day searching for an inpatient that could take him as soon as possible. Many calls later and we were encouraged.

We stumbled upon a wonderful resource called Hope Network. Dane was interviewed over the phone and qualified for a new rehab. Once again, Dane was compliant and resigned as we packed up his bag and drove out to Pontiac, Michigan to a place called Turning Point. On a side street, in a gritty neighborhood, stood this ratty looking old building. One side was for the men and the other side housed the women.

The buildings were separate, but joined-if that makes any sense. The men and woman would be allowed to be together for some free time as well as family visits. This was by far the shabbiest place we had ever gone to for treatment. Like a condemned man, once again Dane trudged up the ramp to the front door. They were expecting us and we were greeted warmly. The intake counselor was a gentleman named Patrick and he and Dane hit it off immediately. Dane was interviewed again and answered the questions honestly.

Patrick explained that a down payment would be expected while he applied for a grant for Dane's rehab. The rules of the rehab as well as visiting hours were gone over with us. All too soon, we were saying goodbye again. Dane gave me a big hug and said, "I love you so much, Mom. Thank you and Poppy for all you do for me." I told him his success in sobriety would be the only repayment I would ever need. With the usual lump in my throat, I drove away but not before promising to see him on Sunday for visiting day. He could call me from the house phone, so I would speak to him before then.

Dane's first call informed me that things were good. He hated the food-no surprise there-and the bed mattresses were like rocks. Well, I told him that it wasn't exactly the Hilton, so what did he expect? They also were having trouble with bedbugs. Great. He gave me his list of things to bring on Sunday and I took notes.

While at Turning Point, Dane made friends with a man in supervisory position. I believe 'Sam' was a counselor. Sam was an older black man and undoubtedly the best dressed man in there-or maybe anywhere. On visiting day, he was sporting a tailored mustard colored shirt with trousers that had a knife edge perfect crease. His alligator shoes were the same color as his shirt. I may add that he smelled delicious.

When Sam entered the room, he and Dane would do a complicated fist bump, hand shake, hug sort of thing. It was decided that they were brothers by a different mother-a fact that I could personally attest to! I sensed that they had connected and Dane confirmed this by telling us of the deep conversations that they shared. I thanked Sam for keeping an eye on my boy. As usual, in treatment, we learned that Dane was a bright boy with natural leadership capabilities. It was even suggested that he could have a future as a drug counselor. Randy and I proudly hung on to those words. Any light at the end of this tunnel was encouraging to us.

Dane ended up staying at Turning Point for three full months and I had high hopes that this extended stay would be the actual 'turning point' for him. I loved that it was a total lockdown situation with the men only going to the store with a house escort. I attended every visiting day and classes that they offered. Randy would join us whenever he possible could and Dane would just light up at the sight of his 'Poppy". They always shared the longest embrace and unembarrassedly, Dane would loudly kiss his cheek. Randy's optimism was contagious and you could just feel how much they loved each other. We headed off to our class and would hook up again later. But, it was getting to the point where we were not hearing anything new. It was the same thing over and over. I asked the class leader if the supporting family lessons in rehab were repetitive, because rehab itself is repetitive?

Addiction is a cycle that has to be broken but relapses are a normal part of that process. She assured me that repeating the lessons are the way they are intended. It takes some time to sink in and apply the ideas for the addicts as well as the caregivers.

On visiting day Dane and I were sitting on a little sofa having coffee and chatting. Presently, one of the female residents came stumbling into the common area. I said to Dane, that if I didn't know better, I would say that she was drunk. She was lurching about and mumbling incoherently. Suddenly two attendants appeared and took the girl by the arms and lead her off. Soon we saw her parents come and take her out of the rehab. Later we learned that she was, in fact, intoxicated. She had broken into a maintenance closet and drank a large amount of hand sanitizer. If that incident doesn't speak of the horror of addiction, I don't know what does. Dane told me that last week a bunch of syringes were discovered hidden in a ceiling tile. Somehow, some visitors had smuggled them in. Hearing this, I squirmed uncomfortably. I was sick and scared to death with this disclosure. I reminded Dane to please stay strong in his sobriety conviction. He promised me that he would.

Another thing that stands out in my mind about that time is that Dane started smoking cigarettes. A former staunch non-smoker, Dane was the first one who cheered loudly when the law passed making it illegal to smoke in bars and restaurants. He hated the smell on his clothes and often got into a rant about the evils of cigarette smoke. I was amused that he didn't consider marijuana joints in the same category. He had even refused to sweep up butts when he was 14 and working in the warehouse. I didn't blame him for the blatant insubordination. In a rehab, smoking cigarettes and 'smokin' breaks' are like a religion. When Dane was at Brighton, he complained that he was the only one left inside when everyone cleared out to enjoy a smoke. Sometimes, if the weather was nice, he'd go outside just to be in on some conversation. Well, it seems at Turning Point, Dane made the choice to get sucked into the hated cigarette vortex. He decided to bum a smoke from a girl he was interested in.

With Dane's propensity to addiction, it took, oh, about three puffs for him to be a smoker. The rest, as they say, is history. I was shocked and dismayed at this new development. And very disappointed. I told Dane how I felt and also that I would never supply him with cigarettes or the money to buy them.

I found this poem that he wrote during this exact time.

Smoking

I watched with growing interest

as she pulled out her cigarettes

She had to look in the jacket

and pat down all her pockets.

Inside there was just the one

she had turned upside down.

Lucky smoke with sarcasm & a frown.

Looking up as the clouds shaded the sun

When she put it to her lips and lit

She explained how she wanted to quit.

That it was more than just a habit

It was something she had to live with.

I told her I'd tried hard to start

But she just stared at me hard.

Then her voice sounded as if from afar.

And here I thought that you looked smart.

She lit one off the other once then twice.

I remember asking why not the light?

27 Club she stated saying it's white

Just don't die she said I might.

Standing together we're quiet a moment.

She asked if you don't smoke, then why come out?

for some reason I told her

I don't know why.

I'm glad I did though, so I guess that's it

When she shivered I offered my coat.

Through chattering teeth, she shook her head no

She spread her arms saying she loves the cold

Chauvinism I told her ain't dead,

just old.

©Dane Jacobs

I thought I had a vague memory of Dane mentioning the "27 Club". Arriving home, I looked it up. Sure enough, there was an explanation. Jim Morrison, Janice Joplin, Jimi Hendrix were among those counted as members-having died as a result of drugs/mental illness at age 27. I hated that Dane and his "smoking buddy" had given the club a rather romantic connotation somehow making a death that young normal.

His treatment went along pretty well, as much as I could tell. He was made a group leader and even moderated at some meetings. He was proud of himself and so were Randy and I. All reports were good and once again he had a little clean time. Maybe a long term rehab was the thing he needed?

I could not allow my brain to ask the obvious question-for how long this time…

Dane-27 years old

One Sunday, I think it was in July, found all three of us at home. With a summer weekend at the house instead of the cottage, Randy and I were taking care of some household projects that had been too long neglected. After a large blueberry pancake and bacon breakfast we were ready to rock. Dane was home for a visit at the time and came up to enjoy breakfast with us. He always loved pancakes and would never mind when we sometimes had breakfast for dinner. After he ate, I said that we could use his help today with some of our jobs. He told me he had nothing special going on and would lend a hand. The yard needed attention and the garage was disorganized-a state that I hated. Randy had plans to power wash the deck as well as the house. Mickey could be counted on to follow us around all day. With Dane's awesome training, he would stay near us, never crossing the perimeter of our lawn. Randy and I went upstairs to change into work clothes and brush the blueberries out of our teeth. Things were shaping up to be a very productive day, and we looked forward to that wonderful feeling of accomplishment and responsibility. A barbeque dinner after would reward our efforts.

Randy went downstairs first and I heard him go out the garage door. Minutes later he bounded up the stairs. "My truck is gone and so is Dane." With that old familiar feeling in the pit of my stomach, I switched gears and wondered aloud what to do next. We started by blowing up Dane's cell phone, which of course, he never answered.

In total frustration, I did the only thing I could think of. I called 911 and reported a stolen vehicle. The sheriff department, by now familiar with our problems, were at the door in minutes. I recognized the officers from past "Dane incidents." As we told our story, the officers were very sympathetic but had to give us the reality check regarding the situation. The fact was, that Dane was residing here temporarily and that changed things. Even without permission the theft was not a crime. We would just have to wait and see if he would come back with the truck. As the sheriff and his deputy left, Randy and I just stood there not knowing which way to turn.

Randy finally said, "Well, let's get in your car and go drive around. We can't just sit here and crawl the walls." I didn't think we had much of a chance, but I went upstairs anyways to change out of my work clothes. We jumped in my car and put the top down for a better view and some sun.

Where to start would be the big question. Randy proposed that we go check out Belle Isle. Dane was crazy about Belle Isle and got familiar with the island when he lived in his apartment that overlooked it. He had spent many hours there with Mickey, walking the beach and hanging out. He loved the fountain and let Mick swim in there, despite the sign that warned that no dogs were allowed. Ever the rebel, Dane had people cracking up watching the antics of a crazy dog splashing around. So off we went down Jefferson thru the beautiful Pointes and into the rougher area preceding the island.

We drove past Dane's old studio at the Parkstone Apartments and I remembered him living there in happier times. I couldn't but wonder if he had been able to stay there, would he have been able to stay free.

As we crossed the MacArthur Bridge to the island, both Randy and I tried to focus on spotting Dane, our truck, hopefully both. On this perfect sunny Sunday, the island was packed with people enjoying soccer games, baseball, basketball, and just hanging out. The air was thick with the mouthwatering smell of BBQ floating from the smoky heat of family reunions and parties everywhere there was a large field or gazebo. Stereos blasted tunes and makeshift dance floors held people of all ages doing the Hustle and other line dances. Plenty of red Solo cups were visible in all areas. There was some sort of classic car club having a meetup and every make and model of car could be seen with their hoods up allowing the engines to be admired. Hot pink, chartreuse, tangerine orange, sunny yellow, metallic purple as well as candy apple red with crazy accessories and large wheels were all lined up. It was quite a sight and Randy and I had trouble staying focused. After several hours of driving around we saw no sign of Dane anywhere.

By now we were hungry and thirsty. Randy suggested that we go eat and come back later when the crowd had thinned down some. Since we were so close to downtown, we decided we might as well go there and relax a bit. Fishbones was the site of our very first date, and we enjoyed the Cajun creations they're famous for. Bread and soup were all I could handle and Randy barely made a dent in his favorite seafood etouffee plate. With a sick dread, I was certain something horrible was happening on the roller coaster. I was afraid.

Minutes later we were back driving across the Belle Isle Bridge to resume our search. The island crowd had cleared out considerably and just maybe we had a better chance of spotting Dane. Warily, we even looked in a wooded area that homeless people crashed in. We did not see him among the little tent city.

Another hopeless hour of scouring the streets left us even more scared and defeated. All that was left to do was go home and wait. There were no words to speak as we drove. Exhausted I went straight up to bed. All day and evening my numerous calls were going right to voice mail and my frantic texts were unanswered.

The next morning following a sleepless night, Randy got up and got ready for work. Over coffee, he told me to try to just remain calm and stay at the ready near the phone. Of course, I would call him if I heard anything. As he drove off in my Mustang, I was stranded at home, pacing the floor, sick with worry. Surely it was just a matter of time before I would hear something— good or bad.

I didn't have to wait long for the expected call. Around noon, the house phone rang and the caller I.D. read St. John's Hospital. I answered and heard a weak voice saying, "Hi Mom, it's me." He went on to tell me that he was in the I.C.U. and could I please come up there as soon as possible? "Intensive care unit?" I gasped. "What the hell has happened? Were you in an accident?"

"No, Mom. I overdosed in Poppy's truck. When I came to, I drove myself here. Poppy's truck is in the parking structure and I am stabilized, but something's wrong with my lungs." I called Randy and told him what had happened. He planned to leave work immediately and come home to fetch me and together we would go see our still broken son. Randy was home in less than 15 minutes and we drove back down to St. John's.

As we pulled into the parking structure, we spotted the truck. Remarkably, it looked no worse for wear. We ran into the hospital and got instructions on how to find the intensive care unit. Going up in the elevator, I could feel my heart pounding out of my chest. I was simply scared to death that the damage Dane inflicted on himself would be permanent this time. Was he ever going to learn the lesson about the dangers of drugs especially opiates and heroin in particular?

As we found and entered Dane's room, what we saw shocked us. He was on oxygen and I.V.'s and hooked up to various monitors. He was pale as a ghost but his big blue eyes were open and clear. The nurse came in and removed his oxygen so he could talk with us. She checked his vitals after we had a moment to hug. Another woman sat in the corner quietly reading and watching everything. I later learned just what her purpose was.

I held Dane's hand, my own "love addiction" taking control, while Randy pulled up two chairs next to his bedside. "Tell us everything that happened" I said. In a quiet voice, Dane told us his story. After breakfast on Sunday, he had an overwhelming urge to use. Because he currently did not have a car, Poppy's truck seemed to be the only option. He knew that if he asked to use the truck we would have certainly been told no. Grabbing the keys off the counter he got in the truck and left. Soon he said, he was overwhelmed with guilt and despair. His old demons that urged him to kill himself were clawing at him full force.

He admitted to feeling like a failure as he was about to use and ruin all of his clean time. The power to stay clean and lead a normal life was never going to happen, in his opinion. He decided to buy enough dope to kill him. He parked on some side street, crawled into the backseat and cooked himself a fix that would surely do the job. He woke a few hours later gasping for breath. Getting behind the wheel, he somehow made it to the hospital.

Upon walking into the emergency room, he was evaluated and immediately transported to the intensive care unit. It was explained to us that he had blown holes in his lungs and they were dangerously close to shutting down. They couldn't believe he had driven himself there. Oxygen and pain meds were keeping his misery at bay. Just then the doctor came by, doing his rounds. After checking Dane's chart, we joined him in the hall for an update. The doctor explained that Dane had seriously harmed himself. It was a miracle that he made it to the hospital alive. He would need to stay in the ICU for a few more days while they gave him treatment to help his lungs heal. We were instructed to keep the conversation to a minimum and let him rest.

He would have a 'sitter' with him at all times, in case of another suicide attempt, giving me the explanation of the woman in the corner chair. It was recommended that Dane be moved to a regular floor in a few days before going back to the E1 for a mental health/detox stay. He then would need another long term drug rehab. There were more questions regarding Dane's health as well as his drug use. Dane's lungs would heal and life would go on, but not without more heartache, there was no hope asked for and none given. This doctor was pragmatic.

As Randy and I re-entered Dane's room, he was quick to apologize. He said he loved us both more than anything and was sorry once again for what he had tried to do. He was sorry for making us worry and he thought he would be helping us to get on with our lives without the constant worry regarding him. He said we would never be free as long as he was alive. He hated what he was doing to us and was sick of himself and his problems. He did not care if he lived or died. Yes, he did not expect to live to have to explain this to us.

He had hoped to die and was surprised when he woke up. His survival instinct proved to have kicked in and somehow he got himself to the hospital. Could we please try to forgive him? He told us the truck keys were in his locker.

Randy and I couldn't comment. We were both just too tired, shocked, and relieved to speak. The intensity and brevity of this was just too much to comprehend without time to process all we had just been through and heard over the past two days. With tears streaming down our faces, we just dumbly sat there. Soon Dane fell asleep and we spoke with his sitter. This gentle woman assured us that she would not take her eyes off of him. She would also help him get his water or call for a nurse to help him use the bathroom. Visiting hours were almost over so Randy and I kissed his sleeping face and prepared to leave the hospital. I told the sitter that I would be back first thing in the morning. Randy and I located his truck and we both drove home. On the way, I called my Mom who was anxiously waiting for our call. It was decided that she would come down for a few days and help in any way she could. She was eager to visit Dane and see for herself that he was okay. She would also call my brother and sister and fill them in with the details. Steve and Lisa would both call me later, very concerned, to check up on the progress.

By 10:00 the next morning, I was back at Dane's side. I sent Randy off to work with a promise that I would call him if there were any changes. He would join me as soon as he got off of work. I brought my iPad and a small blanket to make an eight hour stay more comfortable. I stopped off at the snack bar and got Dane some M&M's. As I walked into his room, I was happy to see that some color had returned to his face. He gave me a big smile and our customary big hug. He was off of the oxygen and said that he felt much better. I asked him what he had planned for himself when he got released from the hospital. He told me that a social worker would stop by soon to discuss his options.

I told him directly that I had to know he would stop this insane quest to 'unburden' us. I loved him so much, even though my extreme frustration, I still could not even imagine a life without him. He needed to realize that we still had hope for his life and would never give up on trying to see him healthy. I feared that if he would die, so would I.

Dane said, "Mom, I love you too but I can't seem to stop hurting you. Nothing is your fault. You did everything right. It's all me. I don't think I will ever feel normal. How do you think my life is going to end up? I'm in pain most of the time, nobody can find a medication for my head and I'm sick of being a guinea pig. And then there is my addiction. It's too much. It's too much for me and it's too much for you. You and Poppy deserve to have a happy life and I will just always bring you down."

What do you say to that, I wondered as I loved and held my sick son?

The next morning my mom arrived to visit for a few days. She was anxious to check on Dane. She barely dropped her bag and I hustled her into my car to go to the hospital. I stopped at McDonald's and got a bag of food for my usual homeless man and he gratefully accepted it. When we finally got up to Dane's room, mom rushed in and hugged Dane hard and long.

"How's gramma's boy?" she wanted to know. "I'm better now, gramma. Don't you worry about me" was his answer. The social worker popped in and asked Dane if it was alright to speak in front of me and my mom. Dane assured her that his information should be available to us anytime we wanted. Her visit gave us a clear idea of the immediate future for Dane. She said they were going to move him down to a regular room by tomorrow once they were confident of the improved condition of his lungs.

Soon after that, he would be moved back up to the locked psych ward E-1 but we would once again be responsible for finding a drug rehab. They wheeled Dane off for a lung x ray and Mom and I went downstairs to grab a bite at the coffee shop. When we arrived back at Dane's room we learned that the x ray looked good and they were moving him to a regular floor. The new room on a regular ward without a sitter was so much less dramatic than the intensive care unit. There were less monitors and he was eating a normal diet and able to use the bathroom without assistance. He even seemed optimistic for the first time since being hospitalized which may have been in part of some new antibiotics, and his now comfort zone of being in a controlled environment. After lunch Dane was sleepy, so mom and I decided to go back home. A quick stop at Kroger and we were loaded up with supplies for a home cooked dinner of our comfort food. Randy loved my mom's casserole dishes and the house would be smelling delicious by the time he walked in. Meatloaf and baked potatoes were on the menu for us that night.

When all else fails, Mom's cooking can go a long way to soothe the soul. In an effort to enjoy the meal, we kept the conversation light. Mom caught us up on all the news in and around Ossineke. Later we all sat in the living room to catch "Dancing with the Stars"-a favorite show of ours. It was a fun escape from our world with all the pageantry and glamour. Mom cracked up laughing as Randy offered his own personal critique of each of the numbers. And he was never far off in his scoring of the dances.

It was a fun evening but we were all exhausted and went to bed shortly after. Mickey joined mom in her room and was his usual bed hog self. Mom generously allowed his company.

Over coffee in the morning, the three of us tried to figure out what the next step would be. I hoped the mental health stay would be long and therapeutic. Meanwhile I would try to find another rehab. The phone rang and I heard Dane say, "Mom, they are moving me up to E-1. I would not be able to visit for a few days, but he had a list of things he needed that I could drop off anytime. He had phone privileges and would stay in touch. "I love you, Mom. See you soon." was his sign off.

I breathed a sigh of relief knowing that at least he would be safe for a while in a familiar place. My Mom stayed for another day and was constantly voicing her concern. Mom, like us was still learning the pitfalls of mental illness and drug abuse. I desperately wished I could have spared her this pain but having been there since the beginning, she deserved to know, Randy and I needed a third party to bounce ideas off of. We recalled stories from Dane's childhood in search of some answers. Mom remembered how Dane would sometimes hole up in his room after visiting his father. I agreed that he was sad, but I don't know if that qualified for an early indication of depression. As a perfectionist, he was obsessed about his homework as well as the organization of his room.

Quirky, for sure but mentally abnormal? I don't know. We could just not find any justification or signs that his childhood somehow was a cause of his condition. His childhood was one of deep love. One time when Dane and I had a session with a new therapist, the question of his relationship with me was posed by the doctor. Angrily, Dane told him that nothing I did was at fault either in his childhood years or even now. Mom would drive back to Ossineke later that day with a firsthand account of things to relate to the rest of my family. I was sad to see her go.

We got very used to the routine of mental health hospital stays. They all follow a basic schedule. With the closing of the larger mental health specific hospitals, regular hospitals were forced to pick up the slack. Dane was housed with every type of problem you can imagine from schizophrenics to eating disorders and everything in between. He was always compliant and never once tried to walk out of treatment-mental or addiction. He was put into a group for therapy that was considered functional.
All of the patients would be together for meals and visiting times. It was during some of these times that we would try to find something to giggle at.

We always felt particularly sorry for the patients who never had any visitors. Family members would sometimes simply give up. Pushed to their limits, they just dropped them off and then picked them up when they were released. Pitifully, sometimes some of patients walked off alone, no visitors coming, leaving us to sadly wonder how on earth they would survive.

I remember one time when Dane was in Cottage Hospital in Grosse Pointe. Upon arriving for visiting day, my bag was checked and I signed in. Also in my hand was a bag containing a cheeseburger, fries, and a chocolate shake. I was then greeted by a very attractive, pleasant woman. She was about my age wearing a darling pink and green print dress that I recognized as a Lilly Pulitzer with matching headband and flats. "Who are you here to visit?" she asked. When I told her that I was here to see Dane she led me to the table where he was waiting. After remarking at what a nice boy he is, she turned and left to assist others.

 After getting my bear hug, I commented that I was surprised to see staff wearing something other than the usual hospital scrubs. Dane busted out laughing as he told me, "Mom, she doesn't work here-she's a patient too!" I would have never guessed that this 'normal' looking woman was getting mental therapy. "Trust me, she's totally delusional." Another time a tall, elegant, black woman strolled by singing at the top of her lungs-beautifully, I may add. Dane told me that she was a member of a famous girl group back in the '60's, and she treated them all to her songs regularly. She also thought Dane was her grandson. On her next lap around she stopped at our table to ask me if I knew her grandson. Dane jumped up and gave her a big hug. He gently explained to her that he was visiting with a friend and would come by to see her in a little while. Satisfied, she wandered off, singing her song.

Dane and I invented our own language that we used at this time. If I asked him who the 'MVP' was, he would know that I was inquiring about the patient with the most outlandish behavior. "So, who is it this time, Dane?" He replied that it was most surely a woman named Gloria. She swears like a sailor and strips all her clothes off he whispered to me. It takes four attendants to get her re-dressed while she shouts out rough profanities. Another woman was a compulsive thief. Not only did she rob from other patient's rooms, she also pilfered all the coffee sugar and straws, as well as the spoons. Regularly they would have to go into her room to reclaim the items and make sure they got returned to their owners. "Don't make eye contact with her" was Dane's advice.

There were never enough attendants to handle all of the outbursts. I know this may seem mean, but we never meant any disrespect and the warnings were for my own safety. Many of the patients were African American and unable to get their hair done, and wandered around with shower caps on their heads. I couldn't help but wonder if the caps looked worse than the actual hair it was covering. One day as I stepped into the visiting area, I saw Dane sitting at a table waiting for me. With a shower cap on his head. His compadres were watching eagerly waiting for my reaction. And I did not disappoint them. With many faces watching, Dane and I burst out laughing as I snatched it off his fool head. He looked ridiculous for sure, but he was willing to sport that cap if it would lighten the mood for a moment. After he was released, I found that very cap in my bathroom at home, where he put it for one last giggle.

This was the relationship that I had with Dane; through thick or thin and 'sick or sin' we used humor and sarcasm to get by. I loved our little inside jokes. A sidelong glance or a pop of the eyebrow, meant something that only we knew. And sometimes you just had to laugh or you might never stop crying. Love is that potent of a drug too.

As Dane was once again released, we decided to try a new rehab. I had heard good things about the Behavioral Center in Warren, Michigan. They would take Dane the next day. Back at home, Dane was once again reunited with Mickey and Jaco. He caught up with Poppy and prepared to go back into rehabilitation. He would be receiving more mental health care at this hospital. I don't remember anything noteworthy about this rehab except Dane remarking that he never really felt safe while in treatment there. A few years later, I think there was actually a murder committed by a patient. While there, they juggled some more of his meds and we hoped that these changes would make a difference in his mental stability. After this short treatment, Dane was released. He came back home and worked for us whenever he felt like he could.

Always stronger after his intense therapy, he seemed renewed and ready to battle. The comfort of the rehab hopefully had given him strength. Always a voracious reader, Dane relied on books and movies as the source of his main entertainment. We haunted used book stores and thrift stores. Dane could spend hours looking at books and would stock up on his favorite authors on the cheap. He also joined the local library. I noticed a particular obsession with the author, Irving Welsh. Welsh, a writer of Scottish descent was very prolific with many titles to his credit. But his greatest claim to fame was the book "Trainspotting" as well as the movie by the same name.

I assumed the story had something to do with trains, which Dane loved as a child. He collected all of his works and seemed to read them over and over. He taped the movie and watched it as if it was on a loop. He was fascinated by it. He could quote the movie and even had developed a passable Scottish accent. He started following soccer always being careful to call it 'football'. He insisted that I shave his head very closely like the lead character played by Ewan McGregor. Reluctantly, I fired up my electric razor. I absolutely hated that look-but he loved it. With his perfect hair line and thick head of hair, I felt the look was very harsh and unflattering. It also made him look kind of thuggish. Luckily, the opinion of friends and family won out and he went back to a longer, more mainstream look. Thank God, I thought as I whipped off the hair cutting cape. At least he appeared normal.

One day, he came bounding up the stairs and into the living room. "Mom, Trainspotting is just going to start. It's so great. What are you doing? Why don't we watch it together?" I wasn't really up for watching a movie right then but he had spoken so highly of this story and he was so excited, that I just couldn't say no. Sighing, I told him okay and we settled in for the flick.

For the next hour and a half I watched in utter horror. This was a gritty tale of heroin addiction that I felt was all too glamorized. It dealt with rebellion, poverty, disease, squalor, HIV, the death of an infant and much, much abuse of heroin. I fully hated the movie and told Dane as much. He said that I probably needed to watch it again to completely 'get it'. Not a chance in hell, I informed him. I had seen enough. But Dane insisted it was a great movie.

I hated that that book, as well as all the others by Welsh that were on display in Dane's library. I promptly erased it from our DVR log and about a year or so later, I persuaded him to do the same. It was simply not a healthy movie for an addict working on his recovery. I had finally learned that we must at least try to eliminate things that trigger heroin use.

Reluctantly, he agreed and even moved on to the "Bourne" series. For a guy who read 'War and Peace' once a year for fun, this "Trainspotting" obsession could not be a good thing.

These changes in an addict's behavior must always be looked for and watched carefully. I asked myself who his heroes were. What else is he watching and reading? What music was he listening to? Is he obsessing over anything else that is troubling? After Heath Ledger died, he became unusually interested in all things Heath. He watched everything Heath ever acted in, and especially loved his portrayal of the joker.

Delightedly he found a movie called "Candy". The movie is a dark and realistic portrayal of a couple who fall into heroin addiction. The flick should have scared the hell out of him instead of fascinating him. He seemed to identify with the star's real life mental illness and turn to drugs. He understood why Heath Ledger did what he did. Dane filled me in on the '27 club'. The classroom lessons from the beginning came rushing back, reminding me of how addiction rewires the brain. I was more than concerned.

Another obsession he indulged in was the book "Into the Wild", by John Krakauer. He loved the true story about a boy who gave away his savings and drove off in his old Datsun. The adventure took him eventually to Alaska where he froze to death in an abandoned bus 100 days later. The story questions roles in society and the conflicts involved in finding your way and/or adhering to traditional rules. Chris McCandless threw off most of his possessions in his quest for enlightenment. I personally liked this story, but not for the same reasons Dane did. He romanticized McCandless's life as well as his death and ideals. He found used copies and insisted that his friends read it. After anticipating the movie of the same title, he watched it over and over. He often spoke of how he would like to put his pets in the car and just drive. I reminded him that with his bad back, sleeping under the stars would not be nearly as cool as it sounds. He accused me of having no real sense of adventure.

"Ha!" You have to be joking. I told him "every day is an adventure in my world!"

Dane-28 years old

Historically, Dane has suffered with insomnia. Even as a child he had sleep issues. Many times around 2:00 a.m. my six-year-old child could be found up watching television or reading. Then he would be crabby the next day unless I could convince him to take a nap. Now as an adult on medication for bipolar disorder as well as extreme anxiety, the lack of sleep was taking on a new shape. Dane would go to bed tired and ready to get comfortable. He preferred something light in the background for white noise as well as a fan. Mickey would join him and the two of them would be snoring in no time. But usually it was a false alarm.

Three hours later he would wake up and be unable to drift back off. He would dig into a book or watch a movie, maybe falling back asleep, maybe not. He was constantly trying to sleep in a normal pattern. He used Sleepy Time tea and it worked-sometimes. Hot baths offered very little relief from the restless leg syndrome that plagued him. R.L.S. is a side effect from anti-depressants and later another script was given to counteract that.

Auntie Cheryl, an expert in essential oils, set him up with her special mix used for sleeping. Always looking for a homeopathic option, he faithfully applied the "sleep cream." It didn't work. He reported that it did help him relax, but again, sleep could not find him. I told him how a meditation that I did would sometimes help me and he promised to try it. Some of his meds would cause nightmares and he would wake up sweaty and exhausted from making war in his dreams. It took time for him to even realize that he had been sleeping. He sometimes would go three nights with no rest and would admit that he saw "shadow people" that terrified him even more. He slept with three horrible looking knives on his bedside and kept three more on a coffee table—just in case. His paranoia increased. He was sleep deprived and that made all of his problems worse. As a result, he slept through appointments and had a hard time going to his N.A. meetings. He became irritable and very hard to reason with. He had very little patience with anyone or anything. I had to monitor his medication so he wouldn't forget or take them twice.

I was just as exhausted as Dane was irritable; I had no time for exercise or simply to work in the yard. I truly felt as if I was losing my mind to Dane's mental health/addiction problems.

Finally, Dane was prescribed Ambien and we hoped that his would finally allow him to sleep.

One night when Randy and I were asleep, at about three a.m. our bedroom light snapped on. Dane was standing there with Mickey. "Get Nonnie and Poppy, Mick. Get 'em!" What the hell? Randy and I woke with a start to see Dane standing there with an odd look on his face. Randy immediately got up muttering, "okay, something isn't right here." I followed him up and all four of us made our way downstairs.

Randy told Dane to sit down on the loveseat and we and sat across from him on the sofa. "What drug did you take, Dane?" It was the only explanation we could imagine for this bizarre behavior. Without answering, Dane got up and walked over to the front door. Opening the door, he stepped out on the porch. Randy and I followed him and watched as he yelled "thank you, come back soon" to some imaginary beings. We gently led him back to the loveseat where he sat down and promptly began pulling on the strings of balloons he was convinced were floating above him.

Randy and I exchanged a worried glance and wondered once again if we should call 911. But he seemed to be winding down and soon would curl up in the fetal position and finally fall asleep. It seemed that he was finally resting peacefully and Randy covered him up with a soft throw. I slept the rest of the night on the couch adjacent to him, hoping I would hear him if he woke back up.

Around eight a.m. I heard Dane stirring around. I watched as he got up and got himself a glass of water. I inquired as to how he was feeling. "Great, why?" I got up and started a pot of coffee. I brought him a mug and told him of his behavior the night before. He listened incredulously. He had absolutely no recall of the crazy events. Again, I asked him if he took his meds properly. Yes, he indicated that the only thing new was the sleep meds he had been prescribed. I grabbed my laptop and read up on Ambien and all of the possible side effects. Apparently, it is not uncommon to experience hallucinatory behavior when using the drug. It just affects everyone differently. Actor Jack Nicholson reported that he suffered hallucinations after being prescribed the drug. After using it the first time he once woke up in his car, parked on the edge of a cliff with absolutely no recall of driving there.

I read a few more stories and did not like what I found. Dane and I decided that he must have experienced a similar reaction. He went down to his room and got the rest of the prescription. Together we disposed of the pills and that was the end of the Ambien experiment.

There was also a night, when again, Randy and I were sleeping. At around five a.m., I was awakened by a steady thumping noise emanating from downstairs on our main floor. I noticed Mickey standing at my bedside, whining. I jumped out of bed and tore down the stairs with Mick at my heels. Halfway between the kitchen and the living room area lay Dane. Clad only in his boxers, he was covered in blood and muttering unintelligibly. A gash on his head was bleeding profusely. His hands were swollen and covered with more blood. It was impossible to see where the blood was originating from. His body was rigid and he appeared to be convulsing.

I screamed for Randy and he came running downstairs. Together we were unable to get him to sit up. He was stiff as a board. I grabbed the phone and dialed 911. "My son is having some sort of seizure." While waiting for the paramedics to arrive, we tried to understand what had happened. Randy stayed with Dane and I went down to his room. I found an unexplainable mess. Danes bedsheets and blankets were covered in blood. It appeared that nothing less than a murder had taken place. Oddly, his weight bench had blood all over it too. What in God's name happened here? I heard the paramedics arrive and ran back up to the stairs and to where Dane was still lying.

The E.M.T. knelt down to ask Dane the obvious question. "What drugs did you take?" Dane mumbled the very unobvious answer, "none." His vitals were spongey enough to warrant medical attention. They loaded him up on the gurney and transported him to McLaren Hospital in nearby Mt. Clemens. We dressed quickly and went to the hospital. Arriving in the E.R., we were directed to Dane's bed. He appeared completely bewildered, but was able to speak a little. In a voice barely above a whisper, he told us that he woke up and was having convulsions. When he tried to get out of bed, he fell and hit his head on his weight bench. He tried to yell but realized that he couldn't speak. He used his bench to try to stand back up, but fell again. He somehow crawled up the stairs and made it to the spot that we found him. When he could no longer move, he tried to hit the wall. His fists pounding on the wall was the thumping noise I had heard. That explained the bloody wall and floor. The nurse came in and advised Dane not to speak anymore and to try to rest. He was admitted overnight for observation.

Randy and I were in shock. What in the hell had just happened? Dane nodded off and we went home. I started coffee and Randy jumped in the shower. When he was done we went downstairs to the basement to assess things. We could not believe how much blood there was all over everything. Dane's meds were on his desk and nothing else looked suspicious.

I called good friend, Rose for help. I explained the situation to her. She has been with us, helping us understand Dane's problems from the beginning. She has driven him to the hospital when he got too anxious to drive himself and once spent a very long night in the St. John's emergency room, supporting us both. Rose said she would come right over and help me clean up his room. Gasping when she surveyed the scene, Rose dug right in.

Together we stripped his bed, and began scrubbing everything bloody with a bucket of hot water and Murphy's Oil Soap. It took pail after pail of fresh water and cleaner to finish this job. We had to trash his ruined rug. I was sick to my stomach, but with Rose's help, we powered through the mess. I don't know what I would have done without her unquestioning help. I am still very thankful and very lucky to have a friend as supportive as Rose.

I got myself together and headed back up to sit with the patient, my only child. Dane was cleaned up and appeared better. The doctors ran some tests but they were inconclusive. They never figured out exactly what happened, but I would be hard pressed to believe that it was anything other than a reaction to some drug. Dane was released the next day bruised and sore, but otherwise alright.

The whole incident remains a mystery to this day. Many situations are still questions with no answers; for me this is a definition of frustration.

I have to admit I was wearing thin from all of the tumult. The ups and downs cycled so fast, I could barely keep up. Randy patiently accepted that I had to do whatever I thought was the right thing. It became very apparent to us that as long as Dane suffered from mood swings—so would I.

Dane's good days became my good days and I, it seemed, suffered almost as bad as Dane, with his bad ones. When he was using, I was petrified every single minute of every single day. It was impossible to sleep. And when he was clean, I was optimistically and cautiously happy. I was riding the rollercoaster, locked in hip to hip with Dane for the terrible ride. I felt that my life was on high alert and I had to be on call 24/7 to do what I could do to help him. The drug of love had become exhausting. Love was my drug, but I was always tired and felt desperate but I didn't know what else to do.

I remember the very first N.A. meeting that Dane went to. He didn't want to go so I said I would tag along for support. We located the meeting, walked in and found seats. When the moderator came to our table, we listened as everyone shared their week. On Dane's turn, he stood slowly and said the expected, "I'm Dane and I'm an addict." Everyone clapped and welcomed him. On my turn, I expressed that I was just there for support.

The meeting was an open one, so it was allowed that I sit in. Introductions were done and some attendees shared the stories of their addiction. A few readings from "The Big Book" came next. Then it came time for open discussions.

Someone at our table asked, "Mom, how are you doing?" "Well, I'm learning. I don't understand how Dane can do what he is doing. We love him and want to see him healthy, but frankly, it's wearing me out." was my reply.

A tiny little girl, no more than 16 years old reached across the table and took my hand. "You need a meeting. A Nar Anon meeting will help you. You will learn to let go. Promise me you will find a meeting." Touched, I told her I would. Over my shoulder I listened in on a conversation. A group of men and women were discussing selling rock salt disguised as crack cocaine in Detroit. I was surprised to hear this. Later Dane told me that most of the meetings had actively using addicts attending. He said you just had to figure out which tables were there for the right reason. Great, I thought. We got through the meeting, but Dane wasn't comfortable. He wasn't ready to share his true life, honestly with strangers. We recited the Serenity Prayer and left the meeting.

It was the last formal N.A. meeting I would ever attend with Dane. He only went to closed meetings after that because he said he was not comfortable discussing his personal life with people not familiar with that way of life.But it appeared that the longer he remained in treatment he appeared to get stronger and more accepting of his and other's addictions.

We also went to a support group for those suffering from mental illness. We were welcomed warmly by the lady moderating the meeting as well as the other attendees. Randy, Dane and I sat at a large conference table, and listened to some of the most heartbreaking stories you can imagine. The gamut from bi polar to schizophrenia and everything in between were conditions discussed. Dane realized that he certainly was not alone in his struggle. When in this setting he willingly shared his story and the moderator and other participants listened closely. Support and resources were suggested. The meeting was very enlightening and we left encouraged.

The pink elephant in our truck after that night was just how very hopeless some of the stories seemed to be and how long the struggle with mental illness could be.

I learned of an organization and shortly after, joined the North American Mental Illness group. They are working very hard for more awareness of the public as well as the government. I get their newsletter and learn about their research efforts. I love reading the success stories from those who are learning to live with their debilitating disease. I hope with all my heart that someday there will be more hope regarding a possible cure, for the full spectrum of mental illnesses. It gives me strength and I am proud to donate to N.A.M.I. regularly.

I would like to try to explain about the relationship between Dane, Randy, and I. I feel like if you knew him better; you would understand why we would do whatever it took to save him. We simply loved him so much. The bond that Dane and I shared was always close. This seemed normal to me-he was my one and only child and the most constant man in my life, other than my Dad. Even my relationship with Randy hadn't hit the 30-year mark. When my 'Great Dane' was born, he became my whole life. We shared tremendous love as well as a strong friendship. Growing up, a boyfriend pointedly said to me that Dane had an Oedipus complex.

Whenever he could, Dane would try to sit in between us or even on my lap. We would exchange a look over his head and make room for little "Odie." When my small son announced that someday he was going to marry me, we would just have to laugh. Poor Odie! But I never minded and was kind of sad when he grew out of that innocence. Never ever, did a phone call or a visit end without an "I love you, Mom." I miss hearing this so very much. Dane was always hugging and kissing me, never caring who was around to witness his true affection for his mom. As a child at school, a college student, and even a warehouse worker-he openly showed his love.

I clearly remember one time when I was visiting him at his college dorm where he introduced me to some new friends. Later I learned that one of the boys remarked about Dane having a 'hot Mom.' Dane, ever the feisty protector, informed the kid that if he ever even looked at me again, he would get his fucking ass kicked. I feel it was a total over-reaction, but typical Dane looking out for me. I counted on him also to be my personal chiropractor. He would rub my shoulders before picking me up and a giving my spine the perfect crack. With great relief, my back would feel much better. Both of us were terrible cuticle pickers, and would slap each other's hands away in an attempt to curb that nasty habit.

Dane's love for Randy was always evident as well. Randy, being the best step father in the world meant the world to Dane. He simply adored his Poppy-the nerdy, cool father figure that accepted him, for exactly what he was.

Randy's love for us was held like a shiny, precious diamond that was faceted in a cut that included support, concern, humor, compassion and above all else love. He was sometimes the only one who could reason with Dane. Quietly and logically, he would help Dane to see the brighter side of things. He selflessly put us first in every situation, supporting and cheering us on. He dove into helping Dane and wholly learned the lessons of addiction and mental illness. He generously paid the huge bills it took for Dane's care.

Many times I cried when speaking to Randy about his horrible luck in hooking up with a damaged package that included Dane and I. He assured us that he wouldn't have it any other way. Dane was so thrilled when Randy and I got together. We were being spoiled and indulged with love and comfort. Dane hugged and kissed Randy freely and lovingly also. Many times over the years during a busy workday, Randy would get a call, "Poppy, is everything okay? Are you and Mom getting along? I don't want to make waves between you two. Please don't be mad at her, Pops. She's just trying to help me." And Randy would assure him that things were fine and he shouldn't worry. "You just try to have a productive and happy day, Dane." Usually an invite for dinner was the next thing they discussed, before Dane signed off with his usual, "I love you, Poppy."

Dane had an affinity for elderly people as well as animals. Even as a child he would visit politely with my parent's friends. He was engaged and open to any discussion. They would get a kick out of this little man child who had no trouble holding up his end of conversations that could include literature, politics and sports. He was comfortable spending time with his paternal grandmother who resided in a nursing home, stopping to say hello to the other patients. My grandparents lived exactly one mile from us in Ossineke. Dane would ride his bike to their house to have breakfast or enjoy an afternoon of cribbage. He loved listening to my Grampa's old stories and giggled when Grandma and Grandpa bickered like The Lockhorns a cartoon about an old married couple drawn by Bill Hoest.

My son loved to watch movies with my parents. He was so happy when he could show them a movie they had never seen, explaining the plot to them as it unfolded. He had learned to appreciate old westerns on my Dad's lap.

As a young adult in Harrison Twp. Dane made unlikely friends with our elderly neighbors. He assisted them in lifting and moving heavy things as well as helping with television remotes and computer snafu's. Recently my neighbor, Shirley showed me something. Well, actually two new things about Dane and his character.

One day Dane was over helping her with a computer problem. She was washing out her coffee pot and lamented at how wasteful it seemed to toss the leftover coffee. Later that day, Dane had knocked on her door. In his arms was a new, one cup coffeemaker. "Here you go, Miss Shirley. Maybe this is what you need." She never used it but keeps it in a cabinet and thinks of him every time she sees it. She then opened a drawer and showed me a piece of paper with Dane's careful handwritten instructions on how to reset her television. She still refers to it when necessary and again, she thinks of him.

He had long conversations with our next door neighbor Dawn and considered this mother of 3 a good friend. They commiserated on some of the same problems they suffered. On the other side of our fence, neighbors George and Jean were also counted as his friends. They chatted over the fence and Dane constantly marveled at how very cool this 80-something couple was.

When Randy introduced him to his future step grandmother an instant bond was formed. She told him endless stories of her childhood and he patiently listened to all her details, asking her pertinent questions that would further jog her memory. Always with a giant hug and his sunny smile, he easily endeared himself. He volunteered at the local library and loved working with the elderly women that volunteered there with him. He charmed the crankiest of nurses when he was hospitalized. Always, just by being Dane, he could make them smile and usually laugh. He often introduced them to me as his 'future wife' or 'future baby momma' and told them "no peeking" under his hospital gown. I often thought that he would be a natural working in the field of geriatrics.

And he loved animals without caution. I recall one day when he was living at Wayburn for the wayward. Even with a bare pantry, Dane was sitting on the porch feeding the numerous stray cats that always hung around. Mystery solved, now I knew where all his tuna went and why it was always on the top of his grocery list.

Once he found a tiny kitten under his car, and scooped up the crying kitty. He simply could not just leave it without any sign of a mother cat. Patiently he fed and cared for Moses by hand until he was strong enough to go to a cat rescue, checking in with the shelter until he was assured Moses had been adopted.

He easily trained Mickey to become the perfect pet for him and us. Dane would get down on one knee and look straight into Mick's brown eyes. He would speak quietly but forcefully and that dog would obey as if he understood English. People still ask me if we have an invisible fence around our yard and I always say, "Nope, just Dane's good training". That dog understood everything he said. When our neighbors acquired a border collie puppy, Dane spent that first sunny afternoon, lying on the grass playing with that little fluff ball. Later when spunky little Sam would escape; Dane was called on to aid in the rescue. After leading his owners on a wild goose chase, a simple command from Dane would have Sammy sitting by his side. It never failed. Recently our friends lamented that they wished Dane was here to train their energetic little rescue pup.

I met a man who was a real Dog Whisperer. When I told him of Dane's skills with animals it was confirmed that he was a natural and a career in dog training should be pursued. When those horrible commercials showing animal abuse come on the television both of us would sit with teary eyes.

Dane, the child of my heart and soul, abhorred cruelty to animals and would have saved them all. It was a dream of his to live on a farm and be allowed all the furry friends he wanted. The animals would have been so lucky to have his gentle, loving care. He just had so much love to give.

Dane-29 years old

Sometime in June of 2012, Dane was back living at Josh House. Abaris revamped their program and we were willing to try the new plan at the halfway house. Supervision was increased along with a tighter schedule of in-house clients. All therapies would be mandatory. The house rules were tightened up and would be more strictly enforced. The men would be encouraged to journal. All meetings were mandatory. Abaris would help them get jobs. There would be more residents as well as more supervision. They initiated a zero tolerance policy regarding misbehavior as well as drugs and alcohol. It was believed that a larger group of residents would encourage the strength in number theory. Hopefully, with the added supervision, this would prove true.

Dane was ready to try again. At this point, I had lost track of the rehabs-both mental and drug that he been in. I can guess that somewhere between 20 and 30 would be a realistic number.

Although Dane tested clean from heroin and non-prescribed drugs during this time, his mental issues were causing much more strain. He would sometimes isolate in his room and not come out for days. He would not answer his cell phone regardless of my countless messages. I would call the house phone and hope for the best. Usually the phone would be answered and a trip up the stairs to Dane's room would be made. The messenger would then timidly step into Dane's room and try to talk to him. Dane would say that he would call me back and usually he did immediately. It truly was never his intention to worry me-but the depression would be so deep that he just couldn't respond.

There were times he sounded so low, that I would get in my car and drive over to offer support, always concerned about his mental health. Entering the house, I would greet the others and then head upstairs to his room. Usually he was lying in bed, staring at the ceiling with big tears silently slipping down his face. I could say or do very little to comfort him. The problems were just too deep and I asked him to double up on his therapy with his psychologist and maybe they could explore some new med options. He was taking his meds properly-they just weren't working any longer

Typically the downward spiral would happen when he couldn't sleep for a few nights. Suffering from sleep deprivation, the slope down would be very short and slippery to his paranoia and depression. The lack of sleep would even further diminish his ability to reason.

Sometimes I would bring Mickey and he would jump up on the bed and lick Dane's tears away. We got permission for him to spend the night and that seemed to help a little. Good old Mick to the rescue. Other times, I would talk him into going out for lunch or coming home for a visit. In a total non-Dane fashion, he would not shower or shave.

I hated to see this because his hygiene was always sure proof of his overall mental state. I would just run out and get him a cheeseburger and a chocolate shake, our shared secret, and pray his old standby would do the trick. On many of those occasions, Mick was the lucky recipient of the cheeseburger that Dane could not choke down.

I hated feeling this helpless and often would appeal to Randy to call him or stop over for a visit. Poppy could relate on a different level than I could and Dane respected everything he had to say. Randy would leave work and the two of them would sit and talk it out. Dane would call me later to say that he felt a little better. I love my husband for so many reasons but especially his own concern and efforts above and beyond he made for Dane.

In June, we decided to go to a Tigers game. I called Dane to see if he was interested in going. He had always been a tigers fan, if he was up to it, it would be a fun night. "Hell, yes, I want to go!" was the enthusiastic response. He got permission for an overnight home visit, packed his duffel and he was on his way.

Recently, my Dad helped Dane buy a car. It was becoming a challenge for Dane to get to the meetings he preferred and he was ready to try to work more hours at the company. My Dad sensed that he had self-esteem issues due to the fact that he was basically grounded. "What 29-year-old does not have transportation?" Dad would argue. I had misgivings.

That freedom also could be trouble allowing him to drive where he wanted. If something triggered an urge, it was a short hop down the Heroin Highway to Detroit. Thicker than thieves, the two of them convinced me of the wisdom of all this. My brother Steve, a Ford salesman, got them a great deal on a used silver Ford Focus. It was in excellent shape and Dane was over the moon.

This left me in a new position as mileage monitor and keeper of the gas money-another role I wasn't dying to take on again. I could only control so much, and I would have to trust Dane's judgement. If he was able to work more hours, he would be able to make the monthly payments to his partner and constant cheerleader— his Grandpa.

On the day of the game Dane showed up at our house in the early afternoon. He looked good all decked out in his Tiger's colors. He threw his arms around me for a giant hug. Mickey came running for his share of affection from his daddy. After foraging around for a snack, we caught up on life at Josh House. The added supervisory attention at the house was a good thing. The current residents were on board in working towards recovery. Our parent meetings proved to us that the program was much stronger. I earnestly prayed Dane's positive attitude would continue.

Randy came home from work early and changed into his Tiger gear. The night was a little chilly and we had to bundle up a bit. Randy suggested that we hit Harbor House downtown for our pregame dinner. It was easy to park on Madison and walk first to the restaurant and then over to Comerica Park. We got seated quickly at Harbor House and ordered our dinner. We were all feeling happy and festive. Dane ordered the lobster mac and cheese and made a gallant effort in decimating the giant platter of it. We chatted with fans at a nearby table that were also heading to the game. All of us were excited to see our new hotshot pitcher, Justin Verlander, do his thing on the mound. When one of the guys inquired about the mac and cheese, Dane handed over his leftover for him to taste. It was a cute and funny exchange between total strangers, bonding over the love for the Tigers. The evening was off to a marvelous start as we paid our tab, and walked over to the stadium. Go Tigers! The usual array of musicians, tailgaters and homeless beggars added to the carnival like scene. Dane begged us out of all of our one dollar bills and donated to everyone he could with gentle words of encouragement and support.

As we located our seats, we were excited to see Justin Verlander warming up right in front of us. We cheered loudly and were rewarded with JV's smile. The game got underway and we made friends high fiving the fans in neighboring seats. A cute couple behind us had a couple of 'fat head' signs. Fat Heads, if you don't know of them, are giant blow ups of someone's face. In this case they were the faces of Verlander and his teammate the consistent Tiger home run king, Cecil Fielder. I admired the utter coolness and perfect clarity of the faces. The girl explained that she worked for the company that produces Fat Head products. Her job tonight was to flash the heads around for as much free advertising possible. However; she was actually shy and not comfortable acting like a rabid fan with the heads. Dane and I did not share her phobia. When she offered us J.V. and Fielder, we gladly took on her task.

We hoisted the faces up and waved them around, sometimes peeking over the side to catch the reactions. Many times we made it to the Jumbo Tron dancing with these foolish things. Normally kind of a shy guy himself, Dane was in rare form and enjoying every minute of the attention. Randy and I loved seeing him so uninhibited and happy. It was a night to remember, and I cherish still every memory from that special night.

On the way home, Dane said, "thank you Poppy and Mom. This might have been the best night of my life." Randy and I were grateful. The tears in my eyes were happy ones.

The next morning Randy was out the door early for work and I headed out for my boxing class. I had been boxing for a few years by this time and I love it. It's probably my favorite way to sweat and blow off steam. Hitting the bag is a wonderful release and great workout. Now if I could just master that damned jump rope!

Two hours later, I arrived home to find Dane up and getting coffee. I was surprised to see him showered and dressed so early. He explained that he had met up with a friend for breakfast National Coney Island-one of his favorite restaurants. I got out all of my bill paying paraphernalia and started sorting out the monthly bills. Dane pulled up a chair at the counter and chatted with me about how fun last night was and how much it meant to him. I loved seeing him so happy. We ended up watching a favorite movie of his after lunch. Afterward, a sleepy Dane decided to catch a little nap before dinner. Later he would be checking back into Josh House. Mickey loyally followed him downstairs.

I spent the rest of the afternoon straightening up around the house. Since Dane would be leaving after dinner, I decided to make his one of his favorite meals. Feeling content, I browned burger and chopped up onion and garlic for spaghetti and a simple green salad with garlic bread were all we needed. Oh, and corn, don't forget the corn. Dane loves corn with his spaghetti.

As dinner time neared, I called down to Dane to come upstairs. Poppy would be home soon and we could eat and visit a bit more before he had to check back into Josh. Dane did not answer, so I gave him 10 more minutes and went to the stairway again. I listened and heard a very odd gasping sound. Oh my God, no. I ran down the stairs to find Dane lying on his bed. His lips were blue as were his fingertips. He was alabaster in color. His face was cold and clammy. Glancing around, I saw it. On his bedside table, the God damned spoon and the needle.

I screamed his name and began pounding on his chest in the area of his heart. I got absolutely no response. I ran back upstairs and called 911. "My son has overdosed. Please hurry." The operator asked if I wanted her to stay on the line, but I needed to try to get his heart started. I ran back down and began pounding on his chest and talking to him. "Dane, c'mon. It's not time yet. Don't leave me. Please breathe." I heard the E.M.T.'s pull in. I hurried upstairs and directed them back down to his room. The sheriff had followed the paramedics in and recognizing Mickey, and gave him a pat on the head.

An E.M.T. asked me if I was sure that Dane had used heroin. When assured this was the case, he pulled a large syringe out of his bag and asked me to stand back. In a scene straight out of 'Pulp Fiction', Dane's heart was restarted by the plunge of a needle. Narcan was injected and almost immediately he started breathing and opened his eyes. I was relieved to tears.

The sheriff asked what had become routine questions regarding the length of Dane's drug abuse. I filled him in as best I could, telling them that Dane was in treatment and had almost a year of clean time. The paramedics loaded him up on the gurney and once again, we were headed off to McLaren for treatment.

Here we go again, I thought wearily. I called Randy and he pulled in the driveway in record time. I shut off all the dinner I had been preparing and together we drove to the emergency room. It was a familiar scene as we parked, walked in, and got directions to his emergency room bed. Pulling back the curtain, we went to his bedside. He burst into tears. "I'm so sorry. I just can't stop." With our own tears flowing, Randy and I reached in to hug him. "I don't know what to do. I just keep disappointing you." he sobbed.

Randy had more words than I did. He gently said that we were not going to give up on him-ever. We would somehow work through this no matter what it took. He had blown his clean time but we could work on getting it back again. Dane morosely wondered aloud, "will I ever be normal again? I am so sick of myself." We stayed for another hour and watched while his vitals were checked and he was stabilized. The doctor wanted to keep him overnight for observation.

Helpless as usual, Randy and I went home. We ate a little but Dane's favorite meal basically went untouched. We were so exhausted from the ups and downs of the past 24 hours that neither one of us could to speak. Quietly, we ended the night and went to bed.

Josh House called in the morning wondering where Dane was. He had not checked back in the previous night. Shit! I forgot to call and give him extra clearance. I explained what happened. Because of the new zero tolerance policy, Dane was again told to leave Josh House until he completed another lock down rehab. Fabulous, I thought. But I was not surprised. Rules were rules and our son would not, nor could not, be exempt.

Dane called early the next morning and said that he would be having a meeting with a social worker at ten a.m. and could I please come? I grabbed a yogurt and got ready for a day with no solid plan in place. Where do we go from here? Should we try to find a new rehab? I was so tired of this fight. I didn't know which way to turn anymore. Resigned, I dressed and drove into Mt. Clemens. Dane looked better. He was finishing some breakfast and cheerfully greeted me, "There's my Mommy!" He reached over the side of his bed and gave me a hug and a kiss. He reported that he had slept well. I asked him the question that had been bugging me since I heard that Narcan gasp.

"Why Dane? Why? You were so happy and had been doing so well. Why?" He knew it was coming. "I wish I knew Mom. I just got the urge. I took back the empty cans and bought a small dose. I hadn't used in so long, that it hit me hard. I'm so sorry."

"Well" I began, "You scared me and Poppy to death. I can't understand you. Do you really want to go back into treatment?" His face dropped as he said, "Mom, I will do anything. Really. I do want to get well. I will get my clean time back." "Well, honey, you have to prove it. Poppy and I are tired and nearly broke trying to help you. And you lost a lot of clean time! Are you trying as hard as you can?"

"I'll do it this time, Mom. I've got the tools; I will do it. I promise."

The social worker had some interesting information. It was finally recognized that Dane needed mental health therapy as well as drug rehab. She said that a dual diagnosis treatment would be what he needed to address both problems. I had been lobbying for such a treatment for over two years now. These facilities are few and far between. I was unable ever to find one with a bed open when we needed it. Out of state facilities didn't seem logical. I located one in California that promised success. It was a year-long commitment with a price tag of $20,000.00.

Again, I was amazed at the uninsured cost of mental health treatment. What other terminal illness would be treated with such ignorance? But, I didn't have time or energy for that battle today. And, we didn't want to be separated. I was thrilled to hear that McLaren was affiliated with such a program and could take Dane immediately, but I wondered why it hadn't been recommended on one of Dane's earlier hospitalizations.

He would spend a week in the mental health ward and then be moved into a drug rehab. Gratefully, I went home and packed his bag. Later he would be released and I would get him admitted to the new facility that was also in Mt. Clemens. The usual procedure was next up, and we filled out all the necessary forms. We hugged goodbye and I assured him that I would be here on the next visiting day. It was odd to feel guilty because I was relieved to have a few days of peace. I needed time to work through the horror I had witness right in my home, again. For a blessed while, I would not be called on to be a lifesaver.

I could exhale while Dane was locked down.

Arriving back home late afternoon, I took a long nap. When Randy got home, we decided to go out to Bath City Bistro for dinner. He was anxious to hear all the updates. Our favorite waitress, Katie, greeted us warmly. "Where's Dane tonight?" she asked. I just told her he wouldn't be joining us tonight. I was just too tired to share the whole story with her. She brought us our wine and I began to fill Randy in. As repetitive as a broken record, I told the tale I seem to have told a hundred times. Randy was happy to hear about the dual diagnosis approach and insisted we have to remain hopeful.

The next two weeks were uneventful, with visits to Dane and his therapists taking up most of my head space. My gym workouts helped me to blow off a little steam and clear my head. I waited by the phone for Dane's calls praying that his voice would sound optimistic.

But the overdose in my basement left me filled with fears and doubts. I had nightmares regularly. I was haunted by the images that I had seen.

Going downstairs for anything proved to be a challenge. Scooping the cat box that we kept down there was absolutely punishing. Half way down the stairs my heart would start pounding out of my chest. I would begin sweating and as Dane's bed came into view, I would 'see' the whole thing again. I was nauseated and close to vomiting. The blue lips...the blue fingers...his cold face...the needle and the spoon—it was all so sickening.

This went on for months. I was so tired from not sleeping well. The dreams were horrifying and frighteningly realistic. Thoughts spun around in my head and gave me bad headaches. I couldn't stop torturing myself with "what if's" What would have happened if I would have waited 5 more minutes before checking on Dane? Could I ever forgive myself? Would I ever feel comfortable in my own home? Would our lives ever be anything close to normal, again? It was feeling like this rollercoaster life was being spent crazily flying in a fast up and down ride. And now the car was coming off of the rails. It was all consuming and I became desperate to find some relief for Dane, Randy and myself.

After a time, I finally was able to work through the immediate horror of seeing Dane almost gasp his very last breath. But I will never forget it. I still hate the basement to this day, but I no longer get sick when I need to go down there. Later, I would learn that I probably suffered from post-traumatic stress disorder. I was used to guilt, anxiety, depression, exhaustion, frustration and worry that came with caring for Dane. P.T.S.D. Why couldn't Dane be diagnosed so easily?

As excited as I was about Dane receiving treatment to address both of his diseases, it didn't take but a moment for the old doubt to be creeping back in. The program was on the right track, but just not long enough. Two weeks was not nearly enough to dig as deep as Dane required for treatment. At this point the addiction was six years old and he had struggled with the mental illness for 12 years. How on earth any professional in this field could be convinced that these two weeks was enough time for such issues spanning years. Again, I could not help wondering if there was another chronic disease that a two-week treatment would be suggested. Ridiculous.

But once again, he had worked hard and the therapists were optimistic. And again, we were told of his cooperation and intelligence. Cool, I thought. Now just fix him please. I never felt that even with the most intensive therapy we were never really understood the root of Dane's issues. Meds were changed and juggled around in an effort to control the symptoms, but to me, all those meds were just band aids. Some of the psychiatrists and therapists seemed just as troubled as Dane was—not a very reassuring thing.

I swear if you ever want to meet an "interesting" doctor-check out a psychiatrist. This observation never failed. But we must keep forging on and doing the best we could. I always asked a million questions whenever I could. I read everything I could get my hands on and still, we were just beginning to learn how to deal with a disease of the brain.

Upon leaving this facility, we learned of a halfway house that was immediately available. It was a 24/7 lockdown situation. The McLaren facility highly recommended this place for a long term follow up. What did we have to lose? What choice did we have? Abaris would not let us back to Josh House and anyway, I was not convinced that they were even the right place for Dane. Dane was released and I told him of the new halfway house.

"No problem, Mom, sounds good. I'm in." We went back home and Dane visited his pets and packed his duffel. After a quick swing thru McDonald's, we were on our way. The facility was a new house; the drive took us all of ten minutes. We followed the directions and were shocked to see a small sign in front of a very nice, modern looking house. We gathered up the duffel bag and knocked on the front door. A very pleasant young woman greeted us. "You must be Dane. C'mon in!" She led us into an office where another woman at a desk looked up and said, "Hello and welcome to the house."

The familiar routine of admission was once again gone through. The woman explained that the residents would not be allowed to leave under any circumstances. Urine tests were randomly timed. There was a total zero tolerance policy for drugs and alcohol. The office was open every day 24 hours a day and someone would always be available to speak with the residents. All meetings were mandatory. The food was provided but residents had to cook the meals and were responsible for the clean-up of the kitchen and dining area. Visitation policy was liberal; just a phone call ahead of time to clear it.

She then got up and invited us to join her on a tour of the place. A very large kitchen had modern appliances and a huge refrigerator. A chart showing meal menus and chores was posted. A big dining table held 12 chairs leading into a large living room comfortable couches and a big flat screen T.V. There was a small, cozy den with bookshelves lined with books. A full basement had a pool table and a dart board. Dane always featured himself a bit of a pool shark and smiled as he took this all in. A weight bench and some free weights encouraged the men's fitness. And best of all, there were three bathrooms-all spotlessly clean, even by Dane's standards. He nodded in amazement with his love for a pristine bathroom! Next up were the bedrooms. Dane would have a small room all to himself-a luxury rarely afforded in rehab. We had never seen a place so well appointed. He set his duffel by his new bed and we were then introduced to his new house mates; four men and surprisingly one young woman. The men all shook our hands politely and expressed a welcome.

The girl stepped forward and said, "You're cute. We're gonna be good friends!" Dane grinned and said, "I'm sure we will!" I shot him a warning look; he caught it and smiled back. Presently a little kitten appeared on the deck outside of the living room door wall. "Look Mom, a kitty!" he exclaimed. Yes, one of the guys explained that she was a feral kitty and they saved a little food for her each day. Dane was delighted and soon made friends with her. I hoped this would help him with his loneliness for Mickey and Jaco. His pets would not be allowed to visit him. Later I would get a call asking me to bring over a box and a blanket to make a little winter house for the kitten. He had me purchase a small light that he would plug in to keep her warm at night. Dr. Doolittle was at it again!

Dane slid easily into the routine of the new house. His room was all settled in and he seemed comfortable. He quickly made friends with two young men who were also addicts. If I recall, one used heroin, and the other one used meth and they both used alcohol. They were old friends and lived their problems together. Both of them had ruined their marriages, lost contact with their children and were ignored by their families. But they owned it.

As I got to know them, I was touched by their regret. The responsibility of their situation was a direct result of addiction and everything that goes along with it. They were unable to keep jobs, chose drugs and alcohol over family, and basically were non-existent in their children's lives. They had failed a few times at rehab, but seemed to be trying hard this time. The streets would be their only option with no family support. Somehow these two homeless men had found this wonderful program that was willing to try to help them.

After sleeping on benches and foraging for food, this place must have seemed like a mirage in a desert of lost hope. Showers, clean beds, and regular meals were luxuries they were never afforded on the streets. Regular therapies were an added bonus. Both men had been clean for 3 months and very proud of it. After a few visits, I soon realized that the guys were always wearing the same clothes. I asked Dane and he said that yes, they had very few personal items. I wondered if they would like a few 'newer things'.

Dane and I guessed their sizes and I made a trip to our favorite Salvation Army and purchased jeans, button down shirts and t-shirts in the appropriate sizes. I added some fleece hoodies and a couple of warm sweaters.

Stopping off at Target, I scooped up some underwear, white t-shirts and socks. Deodorant, shampoo and razors finished up my package. I took home the goods and ran the clothes through the wash. I packed up the fresh clothes and toiletries in two separate bags and made my way over to the house.

A quick stop at Tim Horton's yielded me 6 coffees to go along with a bag of Timbits for their sweet teeth. It took me two trips to transfer in my haul. Dane was not allowed out to assist me. But he met me at the door and took the tray of coffee. "Thank you, Mom. This smells so delicious! Hey guys, Mom brought coffee!" he said as he passed the coffee around. I quietly gave him the other bags of clothes for the guys. Dane put them in his room and would give it to them later in a thoughtful effort to save them some embarrassment.

I sat in the den with Dane and soon the others joined us carrying their coffee. We had an honest heart to heart chat regarding the goals that they set for themselves. All of them hoped for normalcy. I got the idea, again, that Dane was the only resident that got much company. I always seemed to be the only visitor. Just when I thought that I had things figured out, the one girl resident's dad showed up with two large pizzas. He sat the pies down on the table and everyone scrambled to get paper plates, forks, knives, napkins and salt and pepper. He was unable to join us, but wanted to make the effort to treat everyone. All of us thanked him and he was on his way. We all feasted on the hot treats. Dane's new friend looked sad as her father made his excuses and backed out of the door.

Dane and I had some quiet time after lunch. He said that this was the best place he had ever stayed. He loved the women who were on staff to listen to him as well as the therapists. When his insomnia had him up pacing the floors, there was always someone available for him to talk to. The meetings were strong and everyone participated. The program was God based which usually irritated Dane, but now he was amenable. He said he was feeling healthy and whole again. He suggested that we move out to the porch for a smoke and to watch for the kitten. He showed me the box that he had fashioned into a little house complete with my little fleece blanket. If he could have gotten away with it, he would have snuck that little baby into his room. He saved a few pieces of ham from the pizza and put it on the edge of the deck. A few minutes later, the kitten showed up and hungrily munched up the snack. Dane approached slowly and spoke in a gentle whisper, holding his fingers out for her to sniff.

The kitten let him scoop her up and cuddle her in his polar fleece. "Listen to her purr, Mom. She loves to be cuddled. She gets so cold." I sighed and once again bore witness to Dane's talent at taming a feral animal.

The recipients of my little care package were so sweet. On my next visit, they greeted me with hugs and many thanks. They actually twirled and showed me the fit of their new threads. They told me that they were the nicest clothes they ever owned. They were clean shaven. I swear, the smiles on their faces were the most joyful things. I was thrilled to see them so happy. Shyly, again, the men gave me grateful hugs.

It was amazing to see Dane functioning as normal as a grown man could be with a house filled with similar problems, locked up 24/7. Once again he seemed to thrive in this safe environment. The pressure of everyday life was eliminated and the schedule he had to live by was one he could handle. He functioned well under a routine peppered with familiarity and lots of therapy. And I was a short trip away whenever he needed me. I had to try to figure out how to continue this feeling for Dane's life.

3 months later, Dane was ready for release. I picked him up and waited while he hugged the women and all of his house mate's goodbye. "Stay strong Dane", "You got this", was called out to him as we left. I collected a few hugs of my own. "We will miss you, Mom. Take care of our boy!" Dane had a list of phone numbers to call for support as well as all the contacts for his new friends. In rehab, people tend to bond quickly as secrets and problems are frankly revealed.

There is so much commonality with mental health and addiction issues. Usually the residents go from zero to good friend in about 3 days or less. Dane was especially attached to the two guys who were also scheduled to be released. We both worried for their safety and recovery without family support. We would later learn that upon their release, one of them overdosed and died. The other boy was never heard about or from again.

A call to Abaris informed me that Dane would not be welcome back at Josh House. He had fallen off the wagon too many times to be trusted again. He had become a risk to the others trying to get clean. I did not blame them for this. The system they had in place was simply not conducive to Dane's recovery. It just wasn't the right fit. His room had been locked and we could make an appointment to meet there with a supervisor that would unlock his door so we could retrieve his things.

Dane and I were both doubtful that everything would still be there. We drove over to Josh House and made our way up to his old room where we were happy to see that his things were untouched. We quickly loaded everything into my car and left Josh House for the last time.

While Dane was still in treatment we had decided it was time to give him a chance to function on his own. He had learned lots of skills and tools to fall back on. With only a few bumps on the roller coaster he had been mostly clean for a few years. He seemed healthy and ready to move forward. I had been searching for an apartment near our house. I needed to be able to get to him quickly in case of emergency. I still couldn't stand to be far from him. He was not only my heart, but my left arm and I could not function normally without having him on my radar. I read in the Macomb Daily that an apartment complex exactly one mile from our home had openings and was pet friendly. I called and made an appointment to see the place.

The woman in the front office gave me a key and directed me to an available unit. I drove to the rear of the complex and located the apartment. It was in the back area and faced 16 Mile road with large yard and a marshy area in between. The lawn would be perfect for Mickey to run around in. The apartment was 70's style but had been updated. The one bedroom was spacious with a large closet. The galley kitchen was clean and adequate as was the bathroom. He had a laundry room with a small storage area. The living room was small but big enough for a sofa and a recliner. Built in shelves would be handy for all of his geodes and gargoyle collections as well as his books. The carpet was new and the place smelled fresh.

Dane would love this, I thought to myself. Randy was amenable to the rent price and Dane would be able to work to help offset some of the cost. It was our thought that maybe if he got his own place with his pets, he would gain some confidence and self-respect. He had a bridge card and was allowed a whopping 80 dollars a month to put towards groceries. Bridge cards do not cover paper towels, toilet paper, cleaning product, hygiene items or household goods. We would have to help him with those things. But, Dane was not fussy and had plenty of items in storage from his past residence.

We drove home that afternoon and had dinner with Poppy. Dane told him how much he had learned and how good he was feeling. His reunion with Mickey and Jaco was touching. That crazy dog cried and whined and shook his little butt when he saw his 'Daddy' come through the door. The shy little Jaco, jumped into Dane's arms and purred contentedly.

Dinner and a movie made for the perfect evening. We were all together and so happy. If only life would stay like this. We all slept peacefully that night.

The next morning dawned a gorgeous September day. Randy left for work and Dane and I drove the one mile to Willowood Apartments. Dane was so excited to check out this housing possibility. A quick stop at the office, and we were on our way to the back of the unit to check out the available apartment. With an ear to ear grin, Dane wandered around opening cabinets and doors. We decided the place was perfect for him and his pets. There was even a small patio area where he could sit outside and watch Mickey. I was comfortable having him so close to home. In the past, I had made way too many harried drives to check on him. The place was perfectly clean and move in ready. We went back to the office and paid his first month's rent as well as a deposit. We also agreed to a washer and dryer option as well as the additional pet fee. It still was a bargain as far as I was concerned.

The next day, we loaded up his boxes into our cars. I was thrilled to get that mountain of stuff out of my garage. Rose, donated an almost brand new futon and Randy and Dane went out to her house to pick it up. Dane moved quickly and efficiently. He was so excited to unpack his things and set up his new place. I stayed and helped him get his bed made up and dishes organized. Soon it became apparent that he really preferred to do this task himself. Ever the perfectionist, I wasn't doing things right. I asked him if he wanted to work on this project alone and he said, "I would, Mom, if you don't mind. I like to put things in an order that works for me. You go home, you've helped enough. I'll come over for Mickey and Jaco when I'm done."

Okay, I figured as much. Dane had got his television set up and was finding some music to play. He came over and gave me a big hug, "Thank you and Poppy so much. I love you, Mom." I told him that I hope he would use this opportunity to stay on track. We would be in constant contact. Meetings and therapy were non-negotiable. Hope Network has a program that included home therapy visits as well as off-site doctor's appointments.

Dane called Hope and wrote down his schedule for the week. We all felt confident that this was the next logical step. I also insisted on being able to check on things at any time I wanted. Dane handed me over his extra key and assured me that I could come over anytime I wanted. Randy and I would not allow a life of drugs in this apartment. This move was to encourage him to be clean and productive, not a license to use drugs. If we found out that he was using, I would make sure he would get removed.

It would be up to him to figure out where he would go if he made bad choices. If he used and fell off the wagon, I would expect him to be honest and tell us. We would throw him back in rehab if necessary. This was a process, but we would just stay optimistic and keep fighting this beast. He assured me that he was happy and would not fuck things up.

I drove up to Kroger and bought him some basics, coffee, milk, bread, butter, eggs, lunchmeat and Oreos. I also had plenty of things at the house that he could add to this booty. I got dog food for Mickey and cat food for Jaco. Later, Dane came back to our house to have dinner with us. He gobbled it down excitedly. After collecting his supplies, he thanked us both again and invited us to come over and see his progress. So, off we went, including Mickey and Jaco.

It was Randy's first look at the apartment. He was impressed with the little yard and view the place had. When we went inside, we were amazed to see everything put away. It looked cozy and comfortable. I would keep my eye open for a small table for his eat-in kitchen. He had a list on the counter of more things he would need to get set up. Mickey sniffed around and jumped on the bed for a nap. Jaco was snooping about and found an empty box to climb into. Dane proudly showed us everything in his closet and drawers, all perfectly hung and folded. His geode collection was on display on the built-in shelves. A framed picture of Dane and his Grampa held a place of honor. We unpacked the goodies I had brought and decided to get out of his hair. A quick round of hugs and kisses, and we were on our way.

Randy and I drove home and for the first time in a long time, Mickey was not at the door to greet us. He was where he wanted to be-with Dane.

We breathed a cautious sigh of relief and happiness. The gorgeous fall weather was here and Dane was very contented in his new digs. He was participating in his therapy and finally had some clean time under his belt. I surprised him one day and bought him an outdoor rug and two Adirondack chairs and a small table for his little patio. An ashtray and a citron candle were placed on the table. I added 3 plants, a wrought iron sun face and a large metal butterfly. I put solar lights around the top of his fence and voila, he would have a place to sit outside and enjoy his view. When he got home from work, he called me and expressed total delight in his new set up. Apparently other apartment residents had stopped by to admire his set up and he had made a few new friends.

Many hours would be spent sitting out there enjoying his coffee and a smoke-usually reading, with one eye on the ever faithful Mickster, who was enjoying a little sunbath nearby. Jaco watched intently from his perch in the window.

When Dane was living with us, he made friends with a large male cardinal that hung out in our backyard, on the deck. Patiently, he would approach the bird. He carefully put out orange halves for "Mr. C" and spoke gently to him. After a time, Mr. C. would stand on the deck and allow Dane to get about two feet from him. When Dane whispered with the bird, Mr. C would chirp and talk back. It was amazing to see and hear. I couldn't believe how much time that lovely cardinal spent on our deck unafraid of even Jaco and Mickey. Doctor Doolittle-Audubon chapter strikes again, this time in the form of the bird whisperer.

One afternoon, I got a call from a very excited Dane. "Mom you need to get over here right away! You won't believe who is here!" I couldn't imagine who or what could possibly be that amazing to get my son that excited. "It's Mr. C! He found me, Mom. I gotta get some oranges for him. He's sitting on my patio fence right now!" From that day on, I never saw Mr. C on my deck again. His new address was Willowood Apartments.

Also during this time, my Dad was experiencing some random scary symptoms. Always with a voracious appetite, food was suddenly not appealing to him. He was losing weight at an alarming rate. Our usual family Thanksgiving, generously hosted by my sister and brother-in-law was the usual yummy food fest including many of Dad's favorites. Dane and grandpa shared cigs outside on the deck and watched the river rushing by full of autumn colored leaves. Dad had 'quit' smoking years ago, but always held the belief that if my mom didn't actually see him light up, he had quit. He never fooled anyone but we rolled our eyes and went along with the ruse. Dad may have been the only one of us that would benefit from Dane's new habit. Conspirators, once again, they thought they were so sly, but none of us were fooled. But at dinner, something was a little 'off'. My Dad made a small plate and ate very little of it, explaining that he was saving room for pumpkin pie. Usually, Dad looked forward to the traditional dinner, always overeating the stuffing and potatoes and gravy-as did the rest of us. It was a happy and fun day with food, family and football. Dane was in a festive mood and more than made up for his grandpa in the eating department. The day was nothing short of perfect, but I had a niggling feeling that something was very wrong with my Dad.

Later when we discussed this, Dane defended his precious grandpa. "Leave him alone, you guys. You bitch at the poor guy if he eats too much and you bitch if he doesn't eat enough. Stop picking on my Grandpa!" My Dad had been retired for 15 years or so, but worked in his retirement as a courier for cars at the Ford dealership where my brother works. Always a capable driver, my Dad could figure out any direction and route without GPS. He loyally and fearlessly picked up and delivered cars all over the state. He loved to drive and it got him out of my mother's hair a couple of days a week. But Steve was noticing something. Dad appeared tired and maybe a little confused. Steve began booking him less and with shorter routes. Dad insisted that he was fine. He was taking days to recover from one job, sleeping all the time. And he was still losing weight.

Mom took Dad to the doctor for some tests. It was the first week of December when the doctor delivered Dad's results. The test showed pancreatic cancer. Dad was advised to get his things in order and recommended that mom call hospice immediately. Dad would be with us from 9 days to 14 days, max. Stunned, my parents drove home. At one point, Mom asked Dad, what would make him happy. Ever the family man, my Dad answered, "please put the Christmas tree up where I can see it from my chair. I want to eat Christmas cookies and see my kids, grandkids, and grand pets." Done, done, and done.

Randy and I drove up north that weekend to help with Dad. The decline was swift, but we got to spend some time with him while he was still lucid. He ate some of the promised cookies, but you could tell that they didn't hit the spot they usually did. My sister would fix him ice cream sundaes and coax Dad to eat them. For the first time ever, he could eat all the ice cream he wanted, and ironically he could barely enjoy it. Randy helped move Dad in and out of bed and to his chair. Dad's many friends stopped by to visit him for the very last time.

Hospice informed us that Dad's death would be in the next few days. We stayed until the end, with Randy going home to pick up Dane as well as our clothes for his funeral. They came right back to Mom's, and we all prepared for Dad's final days. Dane got to visit with his hero, and was incredibly saddened by his Grandpa's downward turn.

My Dad's passing was peaceful and swift. Hospice and pain meds kept him comfortable as he took his final breath with Mom, Lisa, Aunt Shirley and I at his bedside.

I opened the window, an old Norwegian custom, that allows his soul to fly to out and up to heaven. Brisk December air quickly and surely whisked his spirit off to the heavens. My dad was at peace.

The next day brought a flurry of activity as we prepared for the funeral. Dane was quiet and uninvolved, barely even asking any questions. I asked him to write his Grampa's eulogy and he did. When he read it at the funeral, everyone marveled at his ability to unashamedly express his love for his precious partner in crime. The fact that my Dad was one of his biggest supporters and neither one of them thought the other could do anything wrong was thoroughly reiterated by his very sad grandson. After honoring his Grampa with the heartfelt reading, he came over and hugged me. Sitting down next to me, Dane finally broke down in convulsing sobs and mournful tears.

In a few days, we came back home. Randy had to get back to work and Dane had therapy and doctor appointments. I was ready to get back into some kind of routine as well. I put up our Christmas tree and tried to get into the spirit of the season—my Dad would have wanted me to try.

A few nights later, Randy and I were relaxing after dinner, watching a movie. His phone rang and our Citibank called to approve of a purchase. Seems that our card was used in Detroit recently and a charge of $75.00 was made at a gas station. Randy explained that it was most definitely not his charge. I got up to check our wallets. Oddly, the cards were in place. Still, there was only one possibility to consider. I called Dane and told him that he needed to get over here as soon as possible. Five short minutes later, he and Mickey appeared at the door. "Whatcha watchin'?" he casually asked us. I let him take off his coat and get comfortable on the sofa. "What's up?" he asked. When I asked him if he had used our card, he didn't bother to lie. Yes, I took it and then put it back in your wallet. He explained that he used the card to exchange a tank of gas for cash.

Stolen credit cards used to obtain cash was a common scam that addict's used as fundraisers for their habit. Somewhere deep inside me, I already knew what had happened. "Show me your arms." I demanded. Reluctantly, Dane rolled up his sleeves. Sickly, I witnessed the telltale track marks. Why, Dane why? At this point he had blown his 'clean time' again. He explained that losing Grampa was very hard for him. He wanted relief from his sadness. I told him that was no excuse-stealing and using would not honor his Grampa's memory.

Dane was ashamed and remorseful, as well he should have been. I later learned that a death in the family is one of the most often reasons for a relapse. Poppy and I were very disappointed and disheartened.

At this point Randy and I were throwing our hands in the air. Should we in house rehab again? Should we make him come back home or stay in his apartment? Would we have to guard him forever or was this the time we had to let go? Maybe we were doing too much. I had no answers and was exhausted thinking about the extra control I would have to exercise now that he had awakened his dragon once again.

After a night to sleep on the issues of Dane's giant step backwards, I decided that a family dinner and meeting was necessary. Decisions needed to be made. Christmas was right around the corner and after spending so much time up north, we decided to have a quiet celebration at home-our first without my Dad. I hated the thoughts of this holiday being even more difficult with Dane at a rehab. I didn't have the energy to figure this out alone. Randy and Dane would have to give me their input on the situation. Randy agreed and I called Dane to ask him to come and eat and talk with us later. I think he realized he was under the gun and would not question anything at this point.

With dinnertime set for 7, I went to Kroger for supplies. It was freezing out and I decided that a hot, meaty stew with cornbread was in order. I bought a brownie mix and vanilla ice cream for Dane's special dessert treat. I hoped this would put him in a mood to be totally honest with us. Soon, Mickey was jumping at the back door to get in and I heard Dane 's Docs come clomping up the deck stairs. I collected my hug and kiss as well as a kiss from Mickey. "Mom, it smell's amazing in here. I'm so hungry!" Presently Randy walked in and I got ready to serve dinner. At first we kept the conversation light. Dane asked Randy questions of how his day at work went and Randy filled us both in. Tableside, Mickey begged and I snuck him a few pieces of meat. Dane pretended to protest, but knew it was useless. Nonnie spoiled her "granddog" !

We finished our stew and cornbread. The brownies were cooling on the stove. I got out the ice cream and began scooping up our hot fudge brownie ala mode desserts. Randy was the first to speak. "What do you think we should do, Dane? You broke the rules again. Mom and I will not support you at your apartment if you are using." With a deep breath, Dane explained that he was not in a drug free-fall. He used and it was a mistake. The high wasn't even good. He was sorry and had every intention of living clean. I reminded him that he had almost a year of clean time and he just threw it away.

With the therapy and drug tests through Hope network, he could regain his clean—again. He said that he loved living with his pets in his apartment and he was sorry that he had disappointed us again. He defended himself by saying that he had only relapsed twice in over two years and had gotten control immediately. Yes, that's true I told him but he was playing Russian roulette with his life as well as our patience. I begged him to come to us when he had overwhelming urges and we would work through them together. Randy and I would increase our watch on him. We would demand receipts for anything he spent. Allowances would be spare and completely controlled and I would check his gas mileage. Dane was amenable to these conditions. I however; was not thrilled to reprise my role as detective and parole officer. But, for the first time, we agreed to try to move forward without first completing a rehab.

I finally told Dane that I resented being put into this position again. It was up to him to prove to us that he could turn around and get back on the track. He had one chance. We would try to remain optimistic and give it one more try.

New Year's Eve was around the corner and friends, Kristin and Bob were hosting a party at their home. New Year's Eve has never been my favorite holiday. I've always felt the night was over rated and celebrating with close friends was plenty of party for me. They always hosted great get-togethers that included friends as well as family. There was always and abundance of food and desserts and anyone who dropped by were welcome in their home. The house was decorated festively and everyone was in good spirits. Kristin invited Dane to come over to eat, but he declined and was planning to stay in and watch some movies. I checked with him, and was assured that he had plenty of food for his evening. I hated that he would be alone, but he didn't seem to mind. Isolation had become a common, comfortable part of Dane's way of life. Mickey and Jaco would be by his side. 2012 was a very trying year and I was looking forward to turning that page. I had hopes that 2013 would bring us all some relief. As we ate, drank, and were very merry, I prayed that this would be the case.

At the stroke of midnight, we had a champagne toast and hugs and kisses went around the room. I thought I heard my cell phone ringing and dug it out of my purse, pleased to see that it was Dane calling. "Happy New Year's, Mom! I love you. Put Poppy on so I can tell him!" I handed Randy the phone and the two of them chatted for a moment. Dane was in a positive mood and we were buoyed by the sound of his voice. Soon some pictures came in on my phone of Mickey and Jaco cuddled up contentedly on the couch.

The winter was in full swing in January and February. Snowy and cold, it gave us thoughts of the Keys. Were we comfortable in leaving Dane? How would we manage his care from 5 states away? Friends and family offered to check on him, but the amount of care he was used to was too much for anyone. When he was the sickest, he always needed someone to go to the pharmacy, Kroger, and drive him to his doctor's appointments. Sometimes he would need someone to sit with him through some of his rough low times. I watched constantly for signs of suicide and recognized the ups and downs of his cycles. I arranged with Hope network to have my phone number.

If the therapist that had an appointment at Dane's apartment had any suspicions, they were to call me immediately. My Mom planned to have him up for a visit. Randy would be flying back in the middle of the vacation for 2 weeks, so he would be able to check on Dane also. Dane expressed to us that we needed to get away and assured us that he would be okay. I obtained a schedule of his appointments so I would know if he was making the meetings. His faithful buddy, Tony came and spent some nights with him and the two of them listened to his vinyl and watched movies together. They would eat pizza and re-live happier times. It meant the world to me that this friend, after most others had dropped away, still supported him. Mickey was happy to see his other Daddy. Dane loved Tony and was extremely proud of the success he was enjoying in his professional life.

Blissfully, the vacation went by without a hitch. All reports were good, but both Dane and I were painfully lonesome. We called each other constantly and I mailed him small amounts of cash for groceries. He gave me detailed reports of the pet's activities. His world was so small, but he never seemed to mind it. We spoke of how one day soon he could rejoin us on our vacations; he just needed to get more help and feel stronger before he thought he would want to.

As Randy and I pulled into our driveway returning from Florida that little Focus pulled in right behind us. Dane and Mickey piled out. We all got our hugs and kisses from him and his dog. He looked good and helped us unload the truck. We ordered pizza and enjoyed catching up on everything. I was very proud of him for the tremendous effort he put forward in getting to his appointments, meetings, and holding his own life together. Mickey got some extra ham off of my pizza that night.

Dane-30 years old

As our lovely spring tulips bloomed, so did other problems. Randy's mother Patti had been in remission but her cancer was back. She had struggled on and off with the disease for years, but this time it was spreading viciously fast, everywhere. Being that she lived 75 miles away in Port Sanilac, it was hard for Randy and Mark to be there as much as they would have liked. She could no longer drive and had to hire a driver to help her get to her many appointments. Her sons joined her as often as they could.

After another surgery, the family determined that she could no longer live at home alone. She went into a nursing home for post-surgical care and therapy. Her spirits were good, but it was apparent to us she was fading fast. After witnessing my Dad's suffering, I saw the same signs, and I could see she was slipping away from us.

Visiting her in the nursing home was like a cocktail party without the cocktails! She had so many visitors; her room looked like a chapter of the Port Sanilac garden club which she was a member of. Holding court like a regal queen, Patti entertained us all with her stories from her childhood that she very clearly remembered. Randy and Mark listened intently to the tales that were their history.

Dane, who had a special relationship with Patti, felt horrible. He loved those stories too and would ask her lots of questions. He was always very patient taking in all the details. One afternoon he snuck Mickey, whom she loved, into her room and they sat for hours visiting. He wasn't ready to lose another grandparent.

But things were moving fast. It was soon obvious that Patti would not go home, even with medical assistance. The doctors had done all that they could and advised us to get ready for the end of her life. Keeping her pain free and comfortable were the only options left. We learned of a beautiful hospice nearby and made arrangements for her to be moved there. We barely got her comfortable and she took a turn for the worse. It was advised that the family be called and in a matter of hours she peacefully passed over with her family at her bedside. Dane, who was at home, jumped in his car and joined us. It was a very sad time, yet with her passing went her pain.

In the next few days, the plans for the funeral were made. We chose the most amazing pink and white flower arrangements for her viewing. Randy asked Dane to write one of his beautiful eulogies to be read at the funeral. On the day of the service, he fearlessly stood before a crowded church and delivered a heartfelt and touching tribute, the second time for one of his grandparents. Randy and I were so proud of him. After the service numerous friends and family came up to Dane to express how much they enjoyed his reading. Usually kind of shy, Dane accepted the praise courteously. He appeared to be in good spirits during the luncheon held afterward and even flirted a little with the waitress assigned to his table.

After a very long day, we retired back at the beach house. A bonfire was lit and we enjoyed some family time talking over the day. Dane was somber but engaged. After talking for a while the group decided to do a little tribute. Taking a sky lantern down to the beach, we all gathered around Mark as he lit the candle. We watched with her light as it soared up into the beautiful clear night sky. With the gentle sound of the water and the light breeze we bid Patty goodbye and bid the light up to the heavens. It was a very special moment.

Exhausted, one by one, we dropped off and went to bed. Dane and Mickey quickly sacked out on the couch. Dane has his ear buds in and his laptop showed his music playlist was on. Sometime in the middle of the night, I awoke. Something in my gut felt wrong. I couldn't put my finger on what it was. Getting up, I went into the little living room. Dane looked pale and was breathing loud, ragged breaths. I shook him awake and asked him if he was okay. "Sure, Mom. I'm fine" came the answer. I then noticed that his backpack was on the floor next to the couch.

In a swift move, I grabbed it and unzipped the flap. The look on Dane's face told me all I needed to know even before I looked inside. Stunned there was the needle and spoon. I wanted to know how he could possibly explain this. Sullenly, he said that he was so sad lately, that he just recently bought some dope and had been using again. "Please don't tell Poppy right now, he doesn't need this" was his concern. I told him that I would be telling him in the next day or so. It would be up to Dane to figure out how to cope with this setback.

Exhausted with it all I confiscated and hid his rig, and went back to bed. As good as he'd appeared to have been doing it seemed like we were once again starting over at square one.

The deaths of both Dane's Grandpa and Gramma had triggered relapses.

It's not an unusual trigger, but I was still very disappointed after almost having my son back. On Sunday, we left and headed home to assess the hard choices that faced us once again.

It was decided that we would put Dane back into Harbor Oaks for a chance to get back on his feet. By the grace of God, they had a bed open. Ever compliant, Dane packed his bags and drove to our house. Mickey and Jaco would be on a stay-cation with Nonny and Poppy once again. Randy and I drove him to New Baltimore and got him admitted into treatment. Dane had been to this rehab before, so he knew exactly what to expect. His stay would probably be only for a week, and I prayed it would be enough. Rehabs were not about just 'drying out', but reinforcing the strength of the tools needed to cope with pressure and triggers to use. I reminded him to share with the therapists the difficulty he had in coping with his grandparent's death.

In the past three years, Dane had gotten stronger. Heroin fights a battle that is almost impossible to win. The fact that had been mostly clean for the past two years was something to cling to. It was actually something to be proud of in this screwed up situation. His mental health issues added to the difficulty, but I refused to accept it as a reason for his relapses. He worked hard and immediately seemed stronger. He hadn't used enough dope to have to go through the process of detoxing. Having sat with Dane for a few 'kicks' early on, I was happy he was spared that awful misery.

Soon it was time for Dane to be released. I spoke with his counselor and he was pleased with Dane's progress. "Mrs. Dale, your son is one of the ones who can make it. He's smart and strong. With your family support, he can do this. Call me if I can help in any way" he told me. The repetition of rehab counselors, and doctors was almost laughable. It was simply the same thing, over and over, I could have spoken the words from memory I'd heard them so often.

As we drove through McDonald's, Dane had something to say. "Mom, I'm so sorry for everything. I hate that I keep disappointing you and Poppy. I love you so much, but sometimes I can't help it. Please know that I'm back on track. It's my goal to live clean; whatever it takes."

I reminded him of how many times he has promised that very thing; like the therapists words this to was a repetitive recording that I could recite in my sleep. Dane never lacked sincerity in these promises. Pops and I would like to believe it, wanted desperately to know we had come to the end of this ride, but he had yet to show us his life had turned completely, we had been living off of small victories and accomplishments.

Weary of everything, I had no answer. As we drove back to the house to collect his pets, I hoped for the best but of course, time had taught me to fear the worst.

We all enjoyed the rest of the summer and fall. Dane was feeling better and taking Mickey for walks down the path that ran just outside of his apartment. He would call me later to report how good Mickey behaved and all the cute girls he had spoken with. I was thrilled at any slice of happiness that he could enjoy. He had been seeing a special woman, Michelle, and was on cloud nine with her phone conversations and visits. They spent quiet nights in with Dane cooking dinner for her and then watching movies together. Michelle knew Dane's problems and accepted him along with his baggage. She was there when he needed to talk. Dane expressed to me that he cared for her and felt bad that he didn't have much to offer the relationship.

Don't over think it, was my answer. Just stay healthy and allow her to lean on you, too. I will be forever grateful for the support she gave my son in their mutual affection.

Miraculously, fall and winter flew by without incident. We went to Florida with the same plan as the previous year. Dane was lonely by his own admittance, but remained clean. He was still struggling with depression at times, but he didn't want to try a new medicine. "Better the devil you know, Mom." I continued on believing and telling him that he was responsible for his own happiness. Simply stated, he must find his joy. "Reach out to the family and friends who love and support you, indulge your passions-play your bass, listen to your vinyl's, watch movies, walk Mickey, write your poetry and read."

He was under no other pressure than that. It sounds like an easy thing to do, but with his crippling bouts of anxiety, it was anything but easy. He sometimes could not even walk into Kroger without me or Randy accompanying him. Basic chores at times became insurmountable. Dane would call me crying saying that his apartment was dirty and could I come over and help him. I would drive the short trip and find him sitting on the couch. "I just need you to help get me started." Per usual, after a low period, Dane's mood would swing and he'd emerge on the other side of the pendulum and be horrified at how he'd let things go.

Clothes would be laying around. Plates of half eaten food and empty yogurt containers were on the tables and floors. An overflowing ashtray was on his coffee table. The sink was full of dirty dishes.

The small place could take on a messy state very quickly. If everything wasn't where it should be-it looked like a bomb went off. We opened all the windows to let in some much needed fresh air. I went to work on the dishes and Dane started cleaning his bathroom. Together, we stripped and remade his bed. We folded laundry and started another load. After breaking the back of the job, Dane would send me home. "It's okay now, Mom. I just needed you to help me get started. I can finish things on my own. Thanks for the help. I love you and I'll call ya later." Satisfied that he made it through again I left him and went home.

Springtime was here again I bought new plants for Dane's patio. He still loved to sit out there and enjoy nature. His health seemed strong and he emerged and engaged in everything. We enjoyed many dinners together at our home as well as his favorite place, Bath City Bistro. Most Tuesday nights, Randy and I can be found perched at the bar ordering from the varied menu they offer. Our favorite bartender and waitress, Katie worked there and over the years we have become good friends. We also got to know the chef and he patiently complied with all of my dietary requests. No oil, no croutons, no cheese, no MSG, etc. etc. etc. Bath City, in downtown Mt. Clemens serves as a pleasant mid-week dinner and Randy and I look forward to catching up with Katie as well as some of the other Tuesday night regulars.

When Dane was feeling well enough, he joined us. Dressing carefully and smelling yummy, he would bear hug Katie and join us at the bar. He adored Katie and she indulged harmless flirting. Happily, Dane would converse with her while downing the largest sizzler steak on the menu. Katie would then hook him up with a custom chocolate dessert with extra hot fudge. Another waitress, Corrine, would engage him on the prospects of the Detroit Lions football season. I loved watching these interactions. It was the highlight of his week-and sometimes mine.

Once, when we were in the Keys in August my Dad came down to stay with Dane. Grampa was escorted to Bath City Bistro where Dane would proudly show off his familiarity with Katie and the regulars. And the gang did not let Dane down. Upon entering the restaurant, he was greeted like an old friend. He and my Dad enjoyed a wonderful dinner before heading downtown to catch a Tiger game. Dane's knowledge of Detroit and his navigation around the city amazed my dad. Dane drove him around and showed him some of the job sites our company was working on. Dane parked and together, he and his Gramps entered Comerica Park where they cheered on their team. My Dad spoke fondly of that night where he was treated to some alone time with "the big man on campus". That whole story still makes me smile.

In May, Randy and I were enjoying a weekend up at the beach house. Dane and his pets had plans to join us. When I didn't hear from him on Friday, I started to worry. Saturday morning, I called him and he answered. He told me that he wasn't feeling good and thought he would just stay home. He hadn't been sleeping well and didn't feel like making the drive. I asked him if he wanted me to come home to sit with him. "No, Mom. I'm just tired and need to sleep. Really, I'll be fine and I'll call you if anything changes." I told him to rest and stay in touch.

I hung up and told Randy what was happening. Cheryl expressed disappointment in not seeing him that weekend. She loved Dane and looked forward to the good conversations that they shared. She was a good listener and a friend to him. But now I was concerned. It had been a long time since I had heard Dane speaking so sadly. He sounded unusually down. We made it through the next few days, but I never did relax. I just knew in my gut that something was wrong.

On Sunday, we got home and I immediately tried to reach Dane. After his insomnia periods, he usually slept for days. I didn't want to wake him and left him a voicemail to call me as soon as he was up. On Monday morning, I still hadn't heard from him. I jumped in my car and drove over to the apartment. His car was not there. I shivered to the bone at the possibilities. I feared the very worst.

With a sick feeling, I drove back home. In a matter of minutes, my phone rang. It was Dane calling from McLaren Hospital. Sometime early in the morning, he had a horrible panic attack and was 'seeing things'. His apartment was full of "shadow people". His paranoia took over and he had a panic attack. He somehow had driven himself to a small outpatient clinic near our home. The woman at the counter took one look at him and called an ambulance. He was transported to Mt. Clemens where he was stabilized. I made the familiar drive in record time.

And there he was. Once again, the scenario was complete. Dane was in an emergency room bed with the ugly green robe on. Once in the hospital where everything was controlled, Dane felt safe and calmed down. As much as he hated hospitals, he trusted the professionals to keep him from harm. Dane understood the routine of the organized chaos and it comforted him, every time. I found him lying there, serene as an orchid. "Hi, Mom. Thanks for coming up."

A social worker stepped in and asked Dane some questions regarding what happened leading up to his panic. He answered that he saw the "shadow people" and they were watching him. He feared they would harm him or his pets. They wouldn't leave. He was scared of them and began to panic. His vitals were checked. A doctor came in and went over chart. It was recommended that he be moved to Havenwyck Hospital for mental rehab. Located in Auburn Hills, Havenwyck was a hospital we had never used before. This time a bed was not open, but McLaren wanted to keep him overnight for observation anyway. I stayed most of the day, sitting with Dane and then went to his apartment to scoop up the pets. After dinner, Randy and I went up for another visit. It was more of the same as Dane seemed better and was ready for some help in explaining the shadow people that were haunting him. This is the first time he admitted to seeing things and I was petrified. We had until now, avoided the diagnoses of schizophrenia. Please, I thought, please not that. In my research I had found almost no effective treatment for that particular mental disorder.

Randy and I went home, tired and resigned. This was to be our life. The drug abuse had markedly improved but the mental issues were getting worse. It was a moving target with a bullseye that seemed impossible to hit. Hopefully Havenwyck would give him some added therapy and help with the paranoia that was plaguing him. After another restless night, I got up, had coffee and went to his apartment to get him some things for his stay. The apartment was clean and orderly. I gathered up jeans, T shirts, slippers, boxers, socks, sleep pants and hygiene items. I located the specific notebook that he wanted.

I drove to the hospital. Dane was quietly eating his breakfast. I noticed that he had another sitter in his room. She looked up from her book and smiled. Dane's face lit up when he saw me. "Mom, they are transferring me out to Havenwyck in a while. Are the pets okay with you?" "Well, of course they are", I answered. "How are you feeling today?" "I'm better, but really tired. I swear it's impossible to sleep in here." "Well, hopefully it will be quiet in the rehab and you can get some sleep in there." I gave him his duffel of necessities and McLaren would transfer him by ambulance to the mental rehab. I called Havenwyck and learned that I couldn't visit him until Friday.

I got a big hug and a kiss. I told Dane to just slow down and be patient with himself and others. I tried to convince him that he would be better after treatment and we would work hard at helping him to stay happy. This was just a bump and maybe it could be explained.

Together, we would find his joy. On Friday, I drove to Auburn Hills. It crossed my mind as to how many mental hospitals and rehabs and drug rehabs I had been to. I don't think we missed too many.

I wondered how it would be to have a life without Dane's problems being such a part of my life. Whatever would I do with all of my free time? How much less stress would I have if Dane could just get his shit together? I hoped to someday find out and be able to enjoy my time with a healthy and happy son. It was a goal both of us shared.

After the usual precautions were taken, I was allowed entry to this new rehab. In my hand was a hot McDonald's bag with Dane's treat. I also had a large bag of M&M's for his dessert. They called Dane to the common area and he and I found a table by the window. He still looked tired, but happy to see me. He told me the place was nice and the food was okay with a coffee bar that was always open. One of the nurses was really cute and he told me that they enjoyed a long conversation together. He had been in some group therapies but had not seen a doctor yet, he was scheduled for an appointment later that afternoon. He asked about his pets were doing and I told him that as usual, they were spoiled bed hogs. He smiled weakly. After finishing his lunch, Dane got up and got us both coffee. We sipped it and did our usual evaluation of his compadres.

He filled me in on all the antics but he didn't seem as into our 'amusement' as much as usual. I think he was just sick and tired of dealing with it. He inquired about the rest of the weekend. Poppy and I would pack up the pets and head to the cottage, but would be coming home early to make it to visiting day on Sunday. Dane encouraged me to cut our visit short. "Go home and get ready to go, Mom. I already feel bad about cutting your weekend short." I told him not to worry about us and that the pets were looking forward to some time at the beach. He walked out me out and gave me a hug. "Mom, how am I ever going to repay you and Poppy?" I gave him the usual answer and told him just to get well. We could always work it out.

I drove home saddened by the funk that he seemed to be in. Randy and I packed up the pets and drove north. Just walking into our little beach house was therapeutic for us. As we drove down the hill we could see that Mark and Cheryl already had a bonfire going. We dropped our bags, grabbed a beer and joined them. When we explained Dane's current situation, both of them shook their heads sadly.

Cheryl was the first to speak, "It just isn't fair. He doesn't deserve this. Please tell him that I am praying for him and that I love him very much." I teared up with the realization of how many people loved Dane and prayed for him every day.

Soon it was Sunday and we made our way home. I was anxious to see if Dane was feeling any better. Arriving home, we quickly unpacked the truck and got the pets settled in. Together we drove to Auburn Hills. I got our usual table and Dane came in to join us. "Why aren't you fishing Poppy? Did you come home early just for me?"

Randy answered that "of course I did. Mom and I couldn't wait to see you! And we have stories about your dog. Mickey wore himself out running up and down the beach. We were afraid his fur would catch on fire, he got so close to the bonfire. You need to get well so you can run crowd control on him! So, tell us what's new. How is the therapy going? What did the doctor say?" Dane told us that nothing was really different. The doctor was going to keep him on the same meds.

No real explanation was ever given for his hallucinations. I was as usual, disappointed by the system.

Dane told us that in group therapy he earned the nickname 'Hemingway' for a poem that he had written. He said that he had read it aloud to the group. I noticed that he had a square of paper clutched in his hand. "Is that the poem?" I asked. "Yes" he said, "would you like to read it?" Historically, Dane was shy about anyone reading his writing. He handed it to me and I unfolded it. As I read the poem, tears filled my eyes. It was horribly sad and resigned. Wordlessly, I handed it to Randy and waited for him to read it. "Dane, I don't like this at all. Do you really feel this way?" "Yes, Poppy. I am tired of being a burden on you and Mom. It's getting harder and harder for me to feel good. I love you both and I'm very sorry for everything I've put you through. It would be so much better if I was just gone." It wasn't the first time I had heard those words. "Dane, don't be ridiculous. I cannot live in this world without you. Don't ever think that way. Poppy and I love you very much." All three of us were in tears. I never saw that exact poem again, but among his writings I found a similar poem in a notebook.

COMING HOME

I'm returning home

After seven years gone.

Just a wounded warrior

Who fought and lost a war.

Blindly navigating

To a life left waiting

Across the perilous sea

Whirlpools all around me

Left to my own devices,

Fell prey to the wrong vices.

Life seemed easier

As one of the lotus eaters.

© Dane Jacobs

I understood the seven-year reference as a time table describing his heroin addiction. I did not understand the 'lotus eater' reference. Arriving home, I fired up my laptop to get clarification on that. Through Wikipedia I learned that the lotus eaters were mentioned in Greek mythology. Apparently the lotus eaters were a race of people living on an island near North Africa dominated by lotus plants. The lotus fruits and flowers were the primary food of the island and had a narcotic effect causing the people to sleep in peaceful apathy. It was also mentioned in James Joyce's "Ulysses"-which I know Dane had read.

Monday morning, I got the call telling me that Dane was being released from at 2:00 p.m. At 1:30 I left for Auburn Hills to pick up my 'wounded warrior.' I walked in and identified myself. Dane's therapist came over and introduced himself. He told me that Dane was doing well and he recommended that he continue with treatment and meetings. I could have told you exactly what he was going to say. It was a routine that I knew by heart. Presently, Dane walked out, grinning ear to ear.

"Hiya Mom, lets blow this joint!" By the grace of God, Dane was in a cheery mood. He said goodbye to everyone, and we walked out into the sunny day. He threw his duffel bag in the trunk and we stood outside of the car while he had a cigarette. "Mom, I'm so glad I'm done here. I just want to go home and see Mickey and Jaco." The next stop was Kroger for some staples and then to Rite Aid for his prescriptions. We drove back to collect his car so he could come and get his pets. As usual, Mickey was so happy to see his 'Daddy'. Dane got down on the floor and hugged and kissed his precious companion, while Mickey whined and licked his face. I asked him if he would like to stay for dinner, but he said he was tired and wanted to just go home. Off they went. Please let him be happy, was my prayer.

Tuesday morning, I got up early to enjoy my coffee and crossword before my 9:00 a.m. class at the gym. My phone rang and it was Dane. "Mom, I have a quick appointment this morning and I don't have any gas. Tony called and wants to have lunch later. He's going to be on this side of town around 1:00. Sound good?" Usually, I took him to the gas station myself and used my gas card to fill up his tank. Today, I would be late for class if I did that stop. I would try a new tactic today. Well, I told him, he could come by for some gas money and after his appointment, if he had a gas receipt to show me, I would allow the money for lunch with Tony.

I had a good workout and hurried home after class. My usual yard helper, Tom and a friend, Joe were coming over to trim the two overgrown cherry trees in the front yard.

It was a big job and I was looking forward to having it done. The boys showed up at 10:30 and began work. It was a perfect day to do the job. I planned to do some general weeding while they worked and help haul the branches they felled.

Dane called again to ask if he could come and get lunch money. "Yep, and bring Mickey over. He loves to help with yard work!" I replied. Mick loved laying around the yard and watching us work. It was just too nice of a day for him to be shut up in the apartment. I would send him home later, all tired out. Within a few minutes, Dane and Mickey pulled in. Mickey burst out of the car and started his usual shenanigans. Dane walked over and gave me a big hug. "Here's my gas receipt. I put $5.00 in, just like you told me." I looked over the receipt and saw that he did, indeed, put $5.00 worth of gas into his car. "What time are you meeting Tony?" I asked. "Soon, he'll be calling me when he gets close." I asked him how much money he would need for lunch. "Seven dollars should do it, Mom." I went into the house and went to my hidden stash of bills.

Money and credit cards now lived in a hiding place at my house. I took out seven dollars, exactly. Upon going back outside, I saw Dane shaking hands with Joe and chatting with Tom-whom he already knew. The seven dollars was turned over and I walked him back to his car. "Thank you, Mom. I'll bring you my lunch receipt and tell Tony you said hi." A big hug and a kiss and he was off.

As I walked over to the cherry trees, Joe remarked that Dane was a cool guy. "Yeh he's my boy", I agreed. Two hours later, Dane was back. He showed me the receipt for his lunch. "How was your lunch, babe?" I wanted to know. "How's Tony?" "Oh Mom, he's fabulous. He says to say hi. I'm exhausted and need a nap." He then called over Mick and held the door open while he jumped into the car.

As Dane pulled out of the driveway and onto the street, he slowed the car down to a crawl. "Call me later, Mom. I love you."

Later that night I drove to Mitchell's Fish Market in Rochester to meet Randy and our friends, Steve and Paula, for dinner. I had been calling Dane all afternoon, with no answer. That, combined with road construction, had me in a pissy, worried mood. I was crabby and late when I arrived at the restaurant.

Randy, ever my caretaker, handed me a glass of Pinot Grigio the moment I arrived at our table. "It's all right now, you're here. Relax." Paula said some sweet words and immediately I felt much better.

Dinner was great especially the dessert. The seven-layer carrot cake is a house specialty and we ordered it with four forks. It was no secret where Dane got his sweet tooth from. After dinner, on the drive back across town, I called Dane and left a message to call me as soon as possible. Wearily, I went to bed that night without hearing from him.

On Wednesday, Randy was up early packing a bag for an overnight stay in Lansing. R.S. Dale Company was doing well, and soon it had become prudent to open a satellite office. He would work with his new staff and be back by dinnertime on Thursday. I never minded a night alone. I welcomed the chance to eat popcorn for dinner and to read in bed. Normally, I loved it. But, I was really getting nervous. I went to bed early with a good book but ended up tossing and turning all night.

I got up Thursday morning and made it to my boxing class. Hitting that bag helped me to momentarily forget my worry. But by mid-afternoon, I was sure something was wrong but I was too scared to act on my gut feeling. Since Tuesday, I had felt scared and alone. I called Randy and asked him to come home early. "Dane's not answering his phone. I'm scared to go over there alone. Please hurry." I showered and went to bed. The pain in my stomach as well as my heart was making it impossible for me to concentrate on even reading. Two hours later, Randy was home. He came up the stairs to talk to me. I told him about the last few days and my concern. "Let's go" he said. "No," I answered. "I can't do it. It's bad. I just have this horrible feeling. Please. Just go. Call me as soon as you see him."

Randy got back into his truck and drove the one mile to Dane's apartment. Pulling in the complex, he noticed the Focus parked in its usual spot. Hopefully that was a good sign. Parking and walking down the sidewalk to Dane's place, he could hear Mickey barking. He knocked on the door, but got no answer. In a panic, Randy broke the front window and stepped inside. On the couch, in his boxers and a tee shirt, was Dane. His computer was on his coffee table and music was playing.

Randy went over to him and gave him a little shake. "Wake up, buddy. C'mon wake up." With no reaction, Randy touched his fore head and found it cold as ice. With a mounting horror, he noticed the spoon and needle next to the computer. He broke down crying as the gravity of this situation hit him. Dane was the son that he loved as his own. The son he knew was my world. The son we fought so very hard to save. He realized that somehow he would have to come home and tell me.

Tell me that my beloved son was dead.

At home, 15 minutes had gone by and Randy still hadn't called. I was crazy with worry, and began calling his phone over and over. I texted him asking him to please call me. Soon, I heard him pull back in the driveway and then slowly come upstairs. "God, what a relief" I thought. But then I saw his face, and I knew.

"He's gone, honey. We've lost him. He's gone." In think I remember asking him what Dane was doing. Randy said, "He looks like he's sleeping on the couch, but he's gone."

"Oh, he is not! Don't worry; I know how to wake him up. He sleeps hard, but he'll wake up for me" I said as I pulled on jeans and a tee shirt. Stepping into flip flops and grabbing my purse, we drove like maniacs back to Willowood Apartments. I ran to Dane's door; which Randy had left unlocked. Mickey was very happy to see us. I went over to the couch,

"See, he's sleeping." I touched his face and his arm and realized that he was cold as ice. His fingertips and lips were blue. I took a blanket that was at the foot of the couch and gently covered up my son like I've done a million times.

"Oh, Honey. What were you thinking? How could you, Dane? How can you leave me? After all we've been through, why didn't you call me? We would have gotten through things."

Feeling like someone had socked me in the gut; I fell to the floor, wailing my grief. Somehow, I found my phone and called 911. "Hurry, my son has overdosed." Completely out of our minds, we waited for the E.M.T.'s to arrive. The sheriff and his partner also showed up. They checked Dane's vitals and confirmed what we already knew. Still, I asked what they were going to do for treatment. I was gently informed that it was too late.

"Give him the shot!" I screamed.

"It's too late, ma'am. He's been gone for days." Somehow, somewhere, in my heart of hearts, I knew this was true. Even on Tuesday, I knew. Helplessly, I could only stand there, sobbing. One of the E.M.T.'s recognized Mickey, and patted him on the head. We let Mick out realizing that he had been inside for two days and hadn't even been fed. Poor Mickey. Just then the sheriff asked Randy and I to step outside.

Technically, this is a crime scene, he explained. Numbly, we went outside. Standing on the sidewalk outside of Dane's patio, Randy began calling people. I made the first call to Kristin and she was at my side in an instant. Her hug was all. There were no words.

Seeing the action, Dane's neighbors began walking over to check on things. I explained what happened to them. Shivering, I knocked on the door and requested to be able to get a sweatshirt. As I walked to the closet, I saw my son and looked at his face for the very last time. He still appeared to be peacefully sleeping. Woodenly, I went to Dane's neatly organized closet and grabbed a sweatshirt. It smelled just like him.

Pulling it over my head, I joined the others outside again, and accepted the neighbor's expressions of grief. It appeared that Dane was well liked. One woman with a three-year old son told me that Dane often stopped over to play with the baby. "He could make that child laugh so hard" she told me. Another woman said that he had helped her move in. The young couple that lived next door told me of how he cooked them dinner once to repay them for all the cigarettes he had bummed. Now my phone was blowing up.

Frantically, family and friends were calling to check in. "No, I told them, there is nothing you can do." My Mom, sister and brother promised to come down, first thing in the morning. Mark and Marty would join us on Saturday. Sister in law Cheryl called and for once, was unable to find words of comfort. She was simply devastated.

The door of the apartment opened up and the sheriff told us that we needed to pick a funeral home. All I could think of was Will and Schwarzkoff, in nearby Mt. Clemens. Randy called and made an appointment for the next day to handle arrangements.

In a few minutes we watched helplessly as Dane was loaded into the ambulance.

We went inside and I grabbed Dane's wallet, watch and some jewelry in a small box on the table. I handed these precious things to Randy. I scooped up his kitty and we walked out to the truck. Mickey jumped in, and with crushed hearts, we drove home.

On June 05, 2014, one day before his 31st birthday, Dane had come to the end of the rollercoaster ride of pain and trouble.

Somehow, we got through the night. The realization that Dane was no longer in this world was still impossible for me to comprehend. There was simply no world for me without him. I could not fathom how I would ever go on living. I lay in bed playing my personal memories of him in my head, starting out as an infant and carefully attaching a scene for each of his 31 years. I could barely remember my life before him.

At some point I must have fell asleep. Devastated that this was not a nightmare after all, I woke to Dane's 31st. birthday. My very being was beyond torn, shredded, broken; there is no word for the pain I was enduring. Ripping my heart out would have been less painful. My grief was so complete; I did not know how to fully process it. I had to put one foot in front of the other and I turned to Randy for comfort. He was suffering as much as I was as we hugged and cried wordlessly. Hopefully my family would be here soon and could help place the compass on the right course for what needed to happen.

Dane 31 years old

Soon, my Mom, sister and brother were walking through the door. The looks on their faces mirrored my own. Again, there are no words. Nothing to say and none to hear. We sat down at the kitchen counter and held cups of coffee. My family wanted all the details from the last week. My Mom told us Dane had called her to tell her how good he was feeling and how happy he was to be home with his pets. All of us were in shock.

At 11:00 we had an appointment at the funeral home. Walking into that place was completely surreal as I realized what we would have to do to prepare for Dane's memorial which would be held on Sunday. I was nauseated the whole time. The man in charge was your typical idea of a funeral director. Tall, thin, pale and in an ill fitted suit, he ushered us into his office. I sat at the front of the desk and explained that we would like a cremation and a simple urn. The man left the office for a bit and I remarked that Dane would have hated this "creepy motherfucker", my sister agreed. He came back in holding a form that was for the newspaper announcement. I informed him that I would be writing the obituary myself and would email it over when I was done.

There was no way a stranger would ever write about my son's life. I felt that it would be one of the very last things I could do for him. With things settled, we went down the street to pick out flowers. I was distracted and tired, but the ones we chose were beautiful. Arrangements were made to have Dane cremated the next day.

Randy called our friend Tony and asked him to officiate at the memorial service. Tony is actually our personal trainer, but he is the closest thing to a minister that we personally knew. He graciously accepted and I would send him the readings later after I had time to choose them. He also called Katie from Bath City Bistro to arrange the dinner. Katie told us that she would handle everything, and we were not to worry. She would make sure that all of Dane's favorite foods and deserts would be available.

Dane's friends, Jessica and Ryan, two musicians called. They offered to bring their instruments and play a few songs to honor Dane. I loved the idea. Dane had taken bass lessons from Ryan and admired both of their musicianship. We asked niece Nicole, nephew Justin, and Dane's friend Tony to eulogize him. My friend, Mark Durfee called and offered to write the obit for me, but I told him that I wanted to do it myself. I felt that there was so little I could do now for Dane. Mark spoke to me quietly and logically. His words were a great comfort to me.

The family decided that next Wednesday we'd have Dane's up north memorial luncheon. My sister, Lisa, would host it at her restaurant, Rosa's, and again I was not to worry about anything. She would do him proud, at his favorite place. Kristin stopped by to sit with us awhile. She offered to cancel her family plans for the weekend, but I told her I would be happier knowing they were having fun at their cottage. I know there were others, but I don't remember who. I remember napping. Or at least trying to and then somehow it was Saturday.

Mark and Marty arrived and just their presence was helpful as well as comforting. Dane's buddy Tony came by and sat all afternoon with us in total disbelief that his dear friend was gone. He spoke of the good times they had shared. Neighbor and friend, Dawn, walked in and told stories of her and Dane's good talks. Our friend Pam, showed up with a pan of lasagna. Another friend, Andrea brought sandwiches and a dessert.

I learned first- hand how important these generous gestures are. It was so sweet of them to do that and the worries of lunch and dinner were off the table. More calls from friends and family. I posted on Facebook Dane's obit and details of the memorial. The page blew up with comments. We got out photo albums and chose pictures to put out. It was a painful process, but I was thankful to have something to do. Tony took Mickey for the night. I think I ate, I don't remember. I know I drank wine. Somehow, it was Sunday and we prepared to go and accept condolences, celebrate his life and amongst family and friends say a final goodbye to Dane.

On Sunday, June 08, at 11:30 a.m. Randy and I, Mom, Steve and Lisa, and Mark and Marty walked into Will and Schwarzkoff funeral home, carrying the pictures we had chosen. We were directed to the left where our rooms were set up. Walking into that hushed room, the first thing I noticed were the flowers that were all around the perimeter of the room. I made my way to the table where the urn was. The flower spray surrounding it was beautiful. As the meaning of what I was seeing finally made its way into my brain, the wind was knocked out of me. Never one for open expressions of my feelings, I sobbed freely.

How was I ever going to make it through this day? I would have liked to go home and go to bed, but I could never just leave Dane in this creepy place. We put the pictures around his urn and on the tables.

Within moments, friends started filtering in. My old friend Stacey hugged me tightly. I remarked that we were both members of a club we never wanted to belong to-mothers who have lost children.

She took me aside and handed me a small gift box. I opened it to find a rose gold heart shaped locket, where I could put his picture. We cried with the perfect understanding of each other's pain.

Rose arrived and wordlessly grieving, hugged me tight. Tony, and others that Dane went to college with came in. Katrina generously brought things for coffee and set them up in the room downstairs. Mr. and Mrs. Smykla, who Dane lived with briefly, were early arrivals, thoughtfully bringing food to have with coffee. I hadn't even thought of this. Katrina also had some old college pics I had never seen. I loved seeing these for the first time. Friends from our work came in as well as many of our customers.

I was surprised by family from up north showing up. I knew they would come on Wednesday's memorial, but I couldn't believe they were here now. Two friends from my gym came. Ellen sent a flower arrangement with pet toys for Dane's fur babies. I was touched. My friend Mark Durfee came in. His leather vest, jeans, ponytail, and long beard made for a familiar sight in unfamiliar circumstances. Mark wrote the most beautiful poem for Dane. We had copies made and everyone was encouraged to take one.

Jeannie and others from work came to support their boss and I. Many of them had known Dane since he was 14 and had plenty of stories to tell me. It was a sea of faces, drifting by, in and out giving hugs and sweet words of comfort. Nephews, Dylan and Race drove down from Traverse City to be there. Again, I was touched at the outpouring of love and support.

I am quite sure that funeral home has never seen such a memorial. In the parking lot, a full on tailgating was going on. Friends were having a few beers and shots lifted to the life of Dane. Friend Julie brought me a drink in a paper cup and I accepted it gratefully. Mickey was out there on his leash being walked around the parking lot. Jesse and Ryan came and we settled on a place for them to set up their instruments. I am positive that there was not usually a band in this grim setting.

Soon it was time to begin. We scheduled loosely, the order of which everyone would speak. Linda and John, old friends from our work got up and read a lovely bible verse. Dane just loved John and would have loved his support. J.D. read his reading, telling of childhood memories at the beach house with Dane. He was nervous, but did a wonderful job. It meant the world to his Uncle Randy. Tony spoke of their first meeting at college and their mutual love of music.

Mark spoke first of his friendship with me and then meeting Dane. He complimented Dane on his writing skill. He read his beautiful poem. Dane's gal pal, Michelle got up and told us the story of Dane buying fruit for her pregnant daughter. She was so sweet and I could see why Dane adored her. Niece, Nicole stood up to read next. She paused, shook her head and sat back down. She just couldn't speak. We later learned that she and uncle Mark had lit a sky candle in Dane's honor the night before. She wrote a beautiful poem describing their ceremony. I later made copies for anyone who wanted one. I keep it, along with Mark's poem in frames on the wall of our beach house. Nicole and Uncle Mark are personally responsible for a tradition that will forever be a memory of our Dane.

Then Jesse and Ryan gave me a gift I will forever cherish-the music that they played. With Jesse on her violin and Ryan on his guitar the sweet sounds of J.S. Bach filled the rooms. Air and Arioso made my heart full as I listened. Dane loved classical music and surely would have approved. Next, came Journey's "Don't Stop Believing". They could never have known how many times Dane and I said that very thing to each other. Believe. Hope. Love. When they broke into Guns and Roses, "Sweet Child of Mine," I could no longer remain calm. I cried with a grief I never could have known. It was absolutely beautiful. Tony finished up with some prayers and a blessing. Nobody, but nobody could have missed the love in that room. After thanking all of the friends who made this celebration special, Randy and I invited them all over to Bath City Bistro for dinner and drinks.

We took the flowers and pictures out to the truck. Lisa would take them to Rosa's to decorate on Wednesday. We made our way over to the restaurant, a very short distance away. We had reserved the entire upstairs. Corrine handed Randy and I our usual cocktail. Soon I felt as if I could almost breathe again. I didn't eat and didn't know when I would be able to. Corrine, noticing that Randy and I hadn't eaten, handed us a large carryout for later. Grief filled me up more than any meal ever could. There simply wasn't room for anything else. The last of our guests left the bar about 10:00 p.m. and we were finally able to go home.

On Sunday, everyone left. I moved like a zombie trying to figure out what to do next. His pets were ours now. What about his car, his apartment? I couldn't process anything yet. I couldn't think of the details that I knew would keep Dane right in my eyes, I mostly slept until Tuesday night when it was time to go up north.

Quicksand

Fighting only sinks me faster

it's way beyond my control

impossible to reason with a beast

that's unresponsive to logic

veiled in ambiguity

in a shell of taboo

so familiar to the afflicted

imaginary to everyone else

Living in spite of myself

lends itself to the sole way out.

© Dane Jacobs

Synesthesia

I once had a God

He came and he went

In chains of gold

Lead to the hell he was sent.

My thoughts chime like bells

With synesthesia

I hear and then smell.

©Dane Jacobs

Harmony

Sometimes I feel like

I contain every voice

Or I can create any melody

and remake everything ever wrote

Play beautiful arpeggios

Conduct a piece I could never know

Rhythms guide it all

They multiply and intersect

I hear patterns that are so complex.

I can imagine us all growing

on roots from the same system

Common life source and shared cause

Mandate beyond all harmony

Unquestionably of complete need

We draw life's blood from a pool of complete knowledge.

©Dane Jacobs

Walking into Rosa's on Wednesday, I was struck at the vision I saw. Lisa had set up the urn and flowers and pictures so beautifully. There were large goblets of M&M's on each table in honor of Dane's favorite candy. It was perfect. We had a full house as friends and family turned out to support us. His childhood friends told me stories of Dane. Therese, Brett, Kenny, Allison, Gayle, Graham....all grieving and supportive. I asked my cousin Chuck to say grace and lunch was served. Lisa's staff were incredible. Tracey, Dane's favorite, along with the rest of that wonderful crew had taken care of everything.

My eyes were so swollen that I kept my sunglasses on all day. I was tired, but didn't want the love and memories of Dane to end. It would be the final time that so many people were all loving and thinking about Dane at the same time. It was a very powerful feeling that I could almost reach out and touch. I will never forget the kindness shown to me at that time. Again, we packed up the truck. I couldn't bear to throw away the flowers.

My sister had a great idea as she usually does. She suggested that we go home and get into comfortable clothes. We could grab Mickey and take the flowers down to the beach that Dane always loved. So we did just that. On a blindingly sunny day, we carried the flowers through the sand. Mom, Lisa, Randy, Race and I plodded through the sand carrying the flowers. Mickey ran around while we searched for the perfect place to lay the flowers. I had hopes that birds and bees would find the flowers and do what birds and bees do with them. Maybe they would reseed and come back next year. We placed the flowers off to the side of the main path where they wouldn't be walked on. We held hands and said our personal prayers and wishes for Dane.

We came home the next day to try living our lives without him. I didn't know where to start. I didn't know who I was any longer. What would be my job now? I was no longer a mother, best friend, caretaker, nurse, advisor, parole officer and collaborator with my son-the longest, closest relationship of my life. My role and reason for living no longer had any clarity. Where would I fit now? I mourned the loss of my son, I would never see him lead a full life. I would never see him be in love or get married. I mourned the memories that I would never have a chance to make. I would never have the grandchildren that I had always dreamed of. The hole in my heart was unhealable. And huge. I was changed forever.

I could feel him everywhere and listened for his Doc's to come clomping up the deck. I grabbed my phone with hopes of hearing his voice.

Over and over I played his voicemails listening to the smile in his voice and the "I love you, Moms." My heart stopped every time I saw a silver Ford Fusion. I imagined I saw him in Kroger, browsing for a deal on ice cream. Many times, my random playlist would play our songs. But I had to live. Somehow. Life is about love and hope and I would need to direct that at myself if I was ever to figure out how to go on. Nothing seemed fun or important.

I missed him with every fiber of my being. But I had to go on. Dane would have hated to see me sad. I know he spared me seeing him sometimes when he was down, to save me from worrying about him. One day at a time was a grievous misnomer. One breath at a time was more like it. But as long as he has my heart, there will be love; his love, my love, hope, strength, and courage. The courage to accept that at least I was lucky that I had him for a while. It was my life's work, keeping him alive and happy. For all the pain, suffering and sadness, I would do it all again in a minute. Those 31 years are the most precious gift and I thank God every day that I had his love. It was worth it all. He was worth it all.

I'll love you forever my son, my heart, my brave friend, my love. Until we meet again. All my love. Mom xo

EPILOGUE

That fall, sister in law Cheryl, and I were walking on our beach. She asked me if I had ever considered seeing a psychic medium. Maybe Dane's spirit had a message for me. Really? Yes, she said and it could be comforting to you to hear from him. After all, you didn't have a chance to say goodbye to each other. She had been to a few readings and found the experience incredible. Both times, privately and personally, the medium revealed things that were not easily known regarding departed loved ones. Cheryl had seen Lisa Bousson, a local psychic and talked me into scheduling an appointment. I read that she had this 'gift' since she was a child. Not really knowing what to expect, I called and set up a date for late December. I was allowed one friend as an observer and Cheryl was anxious to go with me. We shall see.

A few weeks later, we drove up north for Thanksgiving weekend with my family. After dinner, my family all gathered outside on a frigidly cold night. You could see your breath as well as every star in the sky. My brother lit the sky candle and I had "Dane's Journey song" playing on my phone. We all watched and listened as the candle filled and floated up to the sky. As the very last strains of "Don't Stop Believing'" played, the lantern floated out of sight. Exactly then, large downy snowflakes began falling from the sky, landing on our upturned teary faces. We could all feel him with us.

On a snowy, December afternoon, Cheryl and I drove to Lisa's house in nearby Sterling Heights. She greeted us at the door and welcomed us into her home. I was a little surprised that she looked completely normal. I'm not sure what I expected. I was nervous as we were escorted to a small cozy office. We took seats on a loveseat with Lisa in a chair across from us. Lisa explained that she has no control over which spirit may show up-she just tells it as she sees it. Many spirits appeared to Lisa and she explained each one to us. First she described an older gentleman that was my Dad perfectly. He was quietly observing with no message for me. Presently she 'saw' a young man with brown hair and blue eyes sitting in the rocking chair to my right. She asked me if I had recently lost a son. Then told me details she could not possibly have known about our relationship. I began to blink back tears. Cheryl and I reached for a Kleenex at exactly the same moment. She told me that he was healthy and happy and out of pain. He wanted me to know that nothing was my fault and he loved me very much. Then she asked me if I knew anyone named 'Joy'. "No" I said, "that name doesn't ring a bell."

Lisa cocked her head to the side a little. "He keeps insisting that you 'find Joy." Tearfully I realized that my son wanted me to move forward and find my joy. It was always our wish for each other and now he was reminding me of it. I could actually feel the warmth of his love in that small room. As I closed my eyes to catch my breath, I could have sworn I felt his arms around me. I will never forget that day and I promise I will search for joy-in my life and the acceptance of his death.

16 months have somehow slipped by. With encouragement from Cheryl, Kristin and my family, I began grief therapy with a lovely therapist, Donna Major. She has helped to accept the loss of Dane and the fog is finally lifting. I'm in a little more control now if anyone asks me if I have any children or when the darling innocent dental hygienist asked me, "How is that sweet son of yours?" At least now I can make it to my car before bursting into tears. It's a process, but I no longer sit on her couch and cry with a giant knot in my throat making it impossible to speak. There are specific steps to go through, although not in a specific order. The steps can be mixed up from person to person. But the old cliché holds true; time does help heal. I'm getting stronger every day.

This summer I planted a memorial garden in our yard, for Dane. Mickey who mourned Dane horribly for months was watching me plant perennials and set up some statuary. I kept all of the statues from his funeral and collected a few gargoyles to add. I found a large glass, red cardinal so 'Mr. C' could be with Dane. I made him a mosaic stepping stone with an old English 'D' in his honor. His grandpa's handmade butterfly house was there to encourage butterflies. At one point, on this hot day, I went in to get a glass of water. When I came back outside, I walked to the garden area and saw Mickey curled up in between the statues and flowers just lying there with his head on his paws. I think he knew that at that moment, he was close to his Daddy.

Writing this book has been a cathartic journey of love, remembering, honoring, and explaining the value of Dane's short, but meaningful life. The mental and physical pain he endured was immense and my prayer is that he is finally released from the torture that was his world.

Because the events sometimes meld into a blur I did my best to figure out some sort of order, based on hospital receipts-most of which I didn't keep after paying them. Dane's volume of writing and poetry give me clues to his mental state although most of the work has no dates on it.

I desperately hope to help someone else facing the mountain of despair that is mental illness and/or addiction. I hope someone will find something of use in Dane's story-he would have loved to help someone.

The simple realization that you are not alone I pray may ease your pain and help you know you never travel alone.

So what have I learned? Somedays the lesson was just survival for our family. It was imperative that Randy and I stay on the same page regarding Dane's health issues and treatment. I learned how very expensive therapy is and that most people simply cannot afford it and never get it. I learned frustration as I imagined an amputee denied his physical therapy. That's how it is for mental illness patients. I learned that our brain is our most complex organ, and extremely tricky to treat. I realized the injustice of insurance coverage being 50% at best.

The same goes for medication. There is not one illness that is so common and life altering but so ill funded and unrecognized. During this time, I joined the National Alliance for Mental Illness, N.A.M.I. Is an organization that is on the forefront of research, awareness and support. I learned that mental illness affects all of us, across the board.

It can touch everyone and you can't always tell by looking, what a person is struggling with. They are not just the pitiful people that we see every day on the side of the expressway or begging downtown at sporting events. Sadly, mental illness is usually not spoken of until a tragic event occurs. Since mostly mental problems do not rear their ugly head until a person is 18 years of age, it is our job to watch for the signs and do all we can do to help, as soon as possible.

A good jumping off point are local, free agencies. A call to the Salvation Army could probably point you in a direction for a possible free program. Hope Network, in our area, was extremely helpful. With both mental health and addiction programs; they helped us cut through the red tape. They found us rehabs and half way houses. It's not perfect-but it's a start.

I am very grateful for Hope Network and all they did for Dane. But it's still an excavation of information. Kind of like a guarded secret that needs to have more bright light shone on it. The internet will be the easiest way for you to find resource treatment in your area. You will wait for call backs as these programs are very busy and usually understaffed. I learned to be persistent. I hope you do too.

As I have previously mentioned, I did not see the signs of mental illness, until Dane actually told me he was feeling helpless and hopeless. Try to watch and listen for any change in behavior. Is he sleeping more or less? Is he retreating from social activities? Is he moodier than usual? Does he seem nervous? Sweating profusely? Speaking too fast or too slowly? It's just any inconsistency or change in behavior. Are there movies, books or people that they seem obsessed with?

You can imagine when Dane graduated and headed off to college that we thought we were out of the woods. But pressure or stress—real or perceived, is the very thing that can set off the changes. Dane put so much pressure on himself but was able to mostly hide the signs from us. Thankfully, our relationship and verbal communication skills were relatively strong. But many do not have someone they can trust with their feelings. Dane hated feeling like a failure and that he let everyone down.

As we learned more, it was easier for us to accept that it wasn't some random character flaw that sometimes prevented him from doing even the things that he loved. Helping begins with baby steps; therapy, education, as well as medication have got to be the go-to for treatment. And more patience than you ever think you can find. You can luck out and have treatment help to stabilize, or move along irritatingly slow with very little progress.

Education, patience, and love will be needed in mountain sized amounts. For years I would fight the battle with anyone who would listen about this injustice. Insurance as well as the general public are hard pressed to recognize mental illness as a "real" illness. But it actually affects one in three people at a rate even higher than cancer.

We have been asked and have donated to many fundraisers for a variety of causes. Not anymore. Randy and I have made a pact to donate to only illnesses or causes that are not covered by insurance. Not one person, ever offered us a dollar to help with Dane's treatment. Mental or drug rehab.

General ignorance prevents total understanding and it was still mostly viewed as all "Dane's choice." We felt very alone in this fight. I've had people say that he just needs to 'pull himself up by his bootstraps!' Or, 'just relax.' Simply do not use. Congratulations dear, you just cured mental illness! And drug addiction too! Why didn't I think of that?

Dane's bipolar symptoms so closely could mock drug use symptoms. So many behaviors cross over. Dane's mania made it necessary to watch his money spending on occasion, but drug use will make him ALWAYS broke. He may ask you for money more often or just slowly begin to steal it. You must always know how much you have in your wallet at any given time. Dane never stole a penny in his life until he began to self-medicate. As the addiction progresses, so will the expense.

Addicts may become secretive about his room or his car. Although I had always honored his privacy, now is not the time to worry about that. It is imperative that you figure out the truth-sooner than later. Time is of the essence. Whenever possible, search these areas. The sooner you can confront the drug use, the better. I had always been able to trust Dane. But self-preservation will become more important to the addict. They will lie because they have to. Drugs will demand more loyalty than you could ever hope to inspire. Watch out for red or 'pinned' eyes. The pupils will appear unnaturally tiny, like pin heads. It is almost a sure sign of opiate use.

It's often hard for them to maintain eye contact with you. I also noticed a dry mouth issue. Dane was always a big water drinker, but at times I could tell he had no normal saliva in his mouth. Movements can be slow and clumsy and Dane would have a hard time sometimes just getting a cup out, pouring his coffee and adding the cream and sugar. It would be painful to watch. Unusual eating of sugar. In addition to eating 5-6 pieces of fruit a day, Dane seemed to always crave candy and sweet baked goods. He would bake a cake and eat the whole thing in three days. He would forage madly for M&M's. Speech can go from chatty to slurring and slow. I could see him sometimes avoiding conversation. It was also common to find him irritable and lacking all patience to handle even simple things.

Dane never had a dripping nose, but that is almost always surely is a sign of drug abuse. And the sweating, always the sweating. He would appear clammy and dripping with sweat. He would wash his face constantly when he was using. Or he would be freezing to death with a big sweater on. Basically, again, any variation from the norm. His eyes may roll back in his head and he would appear to have fallen asleep. In the next second he would be awake. He was abnormally defensive of himself and would seem to have lost his wonderful sense of humor. In retrospect, I would have searched his pockets more frequently. The sooner you can get a jump on things, the more of a chance you have to help the person.

You may even be able to save their life.

I also want to take a minute to dispel the myth that drug addicts and mentally ill people are all on disability. Whether it's Social Security or Disability, they are carefully screened. Dane applied for S.S.D and was turned down. During his interview, it was found that he was clean and articulate and could easily work. The fact of his extreme anxiety was a non-issue to her. He suffered from scoliosis and could not stand for long periods of time. As an addict, he did not take pain medicine and learned to somehow cope with that pain. However, it still affected him almost every day. We were blown away at her ignorance that even with a 3-inch sheaf of **paperwork** with doctor reports and hospitalization records, he was still denied. She told him that he needed to just relax and breathe. (Whoo hoo! Another expert with the cure!)

Years later we hired a lawyer to help us to be awarded some type of help. He was doubtful that he could make a case for Dane. Unlike the people we all know that are on disability that golf and ride four wheelers, Dane could not catch that break. He was left to muddle through on his own. He was one of the fortunate ones that have parents that were able to help. Myth dispelled.

I know that there are still people who think that at least "another drug addict is off the streets. But this is my son that I loved beyond all reason. My grief is no less than if he had died from cancer or a car accident.

Mental illness or drug addiction is rarely recognized as the loss that it is. It needs be remembered that all of these people have identities that are much more than their disease. They are, sons, fathers, mothers, daughters, and friends in short someone's family. I vow to raise understanding and compassion. If you personally are dealing with these illnesses, they will prove to be the fight of your life but in beating the demons back you will emerge, winded, bruised, and much stronger. ALL life is precious and valuable. Don't ever give up on them-there must always be hope—always! You eventually will come out on the other side.

One breath at a time.

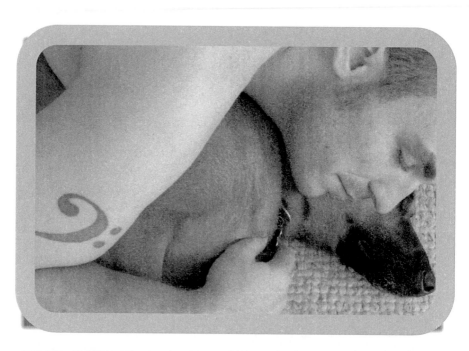

Every star in the sky shines so bright with the beautiful moon.

Not a sound around us, so calm and serene.

Standing on the deck of the ones who loved him the

most and encouraged him day by day.

Holding the lantern with two pair of hands.

Lighting the lantern with strong love while grieving for the

one we will miss but never forget.

Watching the lantern fill with prayers and hope.

"Come on Dane, go go."

To the north it goes.

Flying so high and not stopping...

Clearing the high northern trees.

To heaven it goes, to our great Lord.

We will forever miss that lantern who is our wonderful Dane

but we will never forget him.

Cheers to the thirty years that he lived with those

that loved him and always will.

Rest in Peace our dear Dane.

With love,

Nicole Hogan

SAIL ON

O brother, my brother
of the stormy seas,
waves that ever raged 'neath the calm winds.
You knew, you understood that currents and tides
could any moment take your sails
in directions unbidden.
In having beaten the hurricane;
many times sailed the whirlwind
it was but a slack breeze;
none left to fill your sail,
that you may pass the shoal one more time.
A bend to your keel,
that took you from the shore of living victory
to shores of peace where storms rage no more.

Heaven's door opens,
standing there is my brother,
my brother too soon sailed off
not used to days light
navigator by Polaris' sight.
O brother, O brother gone are you now,
sailed past them beloved by you.
Yet loving you, loving you still.
Your dreams have come to be
the nightmares of a world too dearly paid for
are ended now; escaped.

"Cry not out in the darkness any more"
I hear your soft voice saying
"be still,
be still, listen for me on the breeze of freedom,
I am at liberty, troubled no more."

M Durfee
6.7.2014

AFTERWORD

On a sunny afternoon in October, I had the privilege of sitting down with Capt. Liz Darga and Lt. Daniels of the Macomb County Sheriff's office. I wanted to get a viewpoint from law enforcement that is dealing with the heroin epidemic in our area.

Upon arriving, I was escorted into a conference room and greeting warmly by both Capt. Darga and Lt. Daniels. I was offered coffee and took a seat at the table. I took this time to thank them as well as the whole department that had been to my home as well as Dane's apartment many times. Whether it was an overdose or a mental breakdown that necessitated their visit, Dane was treated patiently and humanely. That kindness meant so much to us all during these already stressful times.

I had my trusty pink legal tablet and pen at the ready. It was at that moment that I realized that maybe I should have put some questions together. But it didn't matter that I was so unprepared. These 28 year veterans were easy to speak to. They inquired about the book I was working on and asked how they could be of help. I filled them in on my goal to help and educate others. The basic facts regarding drug abuse could be found on the internet, but I wanted more personal information. They began talking and answering my questions.

Capt. Darga told me about the Narcan program that was initiated on May 18, 2015. I told her that we had experienced this with Dane and it bought us more time to have him in our lives. As of today, it has been used to save 10 lives in the county. She expressed how maybe those saved could find treatment and also that their families could be spared the horrific grief of losing a loved one to an overdose. Remembering this being our experience, I was happy to hear this. When we moved on to the issue of prevention, she pointed out something I had totally forgotten to remind parents in my early warning signs. A close eye must be kept on your medicine cabinet. Prescription pain killers often can be the beginning of the slippery slope to opiate addiction. Reminding grandparents, who tend to keep old prescriptions is advised also. Remember to monitor your prescriptions and dispose of unused ones. If your child is having a simple surgery such as wisdom teeth removal, a parent should ask for a non-opiate pain killer, such as Tylenol three, avoiding that possible addiction chance. It must be remembered that a large number of heroin addicts do not start with the needle, but rather a legal prescription. The Macomb County Sheriff's office is open 24/7 and will accept and dispose of all surplus meds.

Lt. Daniels firstly discussed the number of heroin overdoses in Macomb County. While it certainly is an epidemic, the number is possibly a bit skewed. The number is taken from the medical examiner's report and not all medical examiners put heroin as the specific cause of the overdose. Macomb County medical examiner does specify if heroin was the case. Nonetheless, he agreed that the numbers were up. Macomb County led the state in recorded heroin deaths from 2010-2012 with a staggering 202 deaths. And the number is only growing. Lt. Daniels went on to explain that the heroin is stronger than ever due to the extreme competition. Smaller doses are needed to cause the sometimes fatal overdoses. We discussed what exactly is being done regarding controlled buys and the busts of drug houses in our area. He told me the basic way that the drugs are moved from Mexico to Detroit and how hard it is to stop these clever systems. Nobody will give up information in the realistic fear that their families would be executed. It is nearly impossible for full penetration in these drug rings. We touched briefly on the issue of human trafficking and the use of drugs in that sad arena. Heroin is used to addict and control the girls. Lt. Daniels gave me his card and offered to answer any questions I may have in the future.

Although I did not speak personally to Judge Linda Davis, Capt. Darga filled me in on some of her programs. April 20, 2015 a government grant allowed for a pilot program using Vivotrol. Vivotrol is an injection that blocks receptors and stops the craving for opiates as well as alcohol for 30 days. By freeing the addicts mind, it allows therapy and counseling to take a better effect. However; some addicts may need 6 months to a year of Vivotrol. At 1000.00 a shot, it will be hard for it to be used as a mainstream therapy.

Judge Davis is also working to educate doctors and dentists on the danger of overprescribing painkillers. It has been proven that these legal drugs, once again, can lead to street addictions. Doctors doling out opiate painkillers are causing so many of our children to innocently become addicted. I must add at this juncture, that it amazes me that these drugs are legal but marijuana isn't. She also founded the Families Against Narcotics group in Fraser, Michigan. After reading this whole site, I feel more educated and inspired by the resources suggested. The personal memoirs and stories brought tears of understanding and sympathy. This support group has grown to 5 chapters in Michigan. Awareness and education as well as camaraderie can be found in great numbers from families who have lost loved ones to drugs. Macomb County is lucky to have Judge Linda Davis as a passionate supporter.

Both Capt. Darga and Lt. Daniels wished me luck with my book. I want to thank all of you that are doing all you can, it means the world to me.

INTERVIEW WITH A FRIEND

Recently, I had the privilege of interviewing a friend who generously agreed to answer a few questions. Chris is a recovering addict that was diagnosed with bi-polar mental illness at the age of fourteen. He started drinking and using various drugs at the age of 13 and started dealing drugs shortly thereafter. His first experience with self-mutilation began at age 13 while he was in school. He suffered anger issues that got him in trouble constantly. He had his first rehab experience by age 16. He has had a very rough time battling this double whammy. He has been through some things that even shocked me-mostly because of how early he started. As Chris sat across the table from me coughing, he told me that the doctor prescribed him cough syrup with codeine. As an addict, he could not take this medicine. He reminded me how many people are addicted to this and that he even knew some kids who had overdosed on it. Chris, like me, shares the goal to help and educate others.

So again, with my legal pads ready, Chris and I went over a few questions that I had prepared.

What is the number one thing you would tell parents to watch for when suspecting drug use?

Chris-Watch for any behavior changes. Anything that seems out of the norm for your child. Don't be too lenient, check in bedrooms and especially cars. But don't be so strict that your child distances himself from you. Do not be manipulated. Don't enable by letting them 'use' in the house. Double check all alibis that you doubt.

What was the hardest thing about your addiction?

Chris-Well actually I can think of two things. Cravings, your mind tricks you into thinking that using is okay. Judgement-peoples preconceived notions about addiction. It is hard being judged. I agreed that the overall ignorance regarding addiction is hard and preventing the understanding needed to properly treat it.

Regarding your addiction, what is your biggest regret?

Chris-Using drugs puts your life on hold.

How did your bi-polar affect your drug use?

Chris-My anger made me reason out using drugs.

What is your proudest moment?

Chris-Staying clean and holding down a job that provides stability. Also making my family proud of me.

What do you wish you would have done differently?

Chris-I wish I never would have started using opiates. Just never would have picked 'em up.

What was your very lowest moment?

Chris-Well, that would be saving my girlfriends life with C.P.R. after an overdose. Realizing I was at the bottom-poor, addicted, homeless and sick and tired. I just wanted to get clean.

What are you most ashamed of?

Chris-How much I hurt and disrespected my family. My little sister once told me that she couldn't fall asleep until I got home because she was scared that I might be dead. Hearing her say that just broke me. I felt so bad and could not stop crying when I heard this.

Proudest moment?

Chris-I am proudest of the maintenance of my sobriety. Also that I gained back family support and trust. I'm proud that I'm not hurting myself or others.

Any advice for someone suffering with addiction?

Chris-There are people who can help and understand you. Don't be afraid to ask for help. Admit that you need help. Realize that in the drug world, respect is false. You are never respected— only used. Respect is earned and comes with living a respectful life. Do not fall for the glamorization of drugs, they will eventually take everything you love. You will be unable to maintain and will end up locked up or dead.

How do you feel today?

Chris-Hopeful and proud to be living a responsible life. I have respect from family and friends. I enjoy spending time with my girlfriend and even going to church. There is a minister that I can talk to. **Chris and I finished dinner, hugged and vowed to stay in touch. As he walked away, I said a silent prayer that he would continue on this journey. I will do all I can to support his effort.**

Rest Peacefully My Love

Made in the USA
Middletown, DE
06 July 2016